Falling in Love with Work

A Practical Guide to Igniting Your Passion for Your Career

Denice Kronau

Published by Wheatmark®
610 East Delano Street, Suite 104
Tucson, Arizona 85705 U.S.A.
www.wheatmark.com

ISBN: 978-1-60494-566-9
LCCN: 2011922922

Back cover photo credit: Cary Hazlegrove

Book cover design: Monkey C Media

For my husband, Michael

Contents

Acknowledgments

Many people encouraged me as I wrote this book, and without their help it would not exist. Two work colleagues, Karen Kalina and Jim Holtje, introduced me to Mary Albon and Bert Holtje; with these introductions, I was on my way! I owe so much to my writing coach and editor, Mary Albon. Mary always knew how to keep me on track, be it with humor, logic, or that extra push to rewrite something that I thought was perfect. Mary motivated me to keep writing, even when I started doubting whether I had something to say that was worth putting down on paper. Any errors in this book are definitely my own. I would also like to thank Bert Holtje, who was the very first publishing executive who told me I could write and who encouraged me to continue with my project. Bert's industry knowledge led me to Penny Sansevieri at Author Marketing Experts, who led me to Jennifer Thompson and her team at Monkey C Media, and to Grael Norton, Lori Leavitt, and the team at Wheatmark Publishing. This publishing dream team translated my vision into the book you hold in your hands. I was honored to work with each of them, especially as a first-time author.

Dr. Michael Phelps, the Norton Simon professor and chair of the Molecular and Medical Pharmacology Department at UCLA, was the catalyst for my recovery from work burnout. During one magical summer, Mike and I developed an online friendship that sustained me through the sometimes painful process of rediscovery. Our nearly daily emails served as a GPS to my new life and provided much of the content for this book. While it's not nearly as iconic as Bogart's famous line in the movie *Casablanca*, "We'll always have Paris," I will always have my "Summer of Mike," which helped me find my way back to the work I love and to this book.

I am quite sure my friend Marybeth Gibson believed in this book more than I did at times! Her support, encouragement, and excitement about the project motivated me during the long months of writing, rewriting, and yes, rewriting again.

I would like to thank Klaus Stegemann, who extended to me the lifeline of a sabbatical when I was prepared to throw my career away. More than being my boss, he was my friend during a very difficult time.

I would also like to thank the many colleagues who walked beside me as I learned all of these lessons and who created a community that I realized I wanted to return to. The desire to rejoin you inspired me to recover.

My family, and especially my parents, Larry and Dee Kronau, have always given me love, support, and encouragement. They taught me that work is important, but I always knew that whether I was a CEO or a Starbucks barista, it only mattered to them that I was happy.

Lynn Krill has been my friend for nearly forty years and has been with me every step of the way. Mike Phelps once described his relationship with his boxing coach, Ira, like this: "He was not only on my side, but also by my side." This best describes my relationship with Lynn. I count myself very lucky to have her in my life.

But above all, I am grateful to my husband, Michael Reitermann. When I could not work one more day, his unconditional love and support created the safe harbor where I could escape the stormy seas of my work life. It is thanks to him that I was able to recover. And without his loving encouragement and faith in me, this book would not exist.

Introduction

From the Corner Office to the Beach and Back Again

If you are feeling trapped and unhappy at work, or if you are out of a job, I have a story that might help you get some perspective back in your life. A few years ago when the economy was going gangbusters, I was completely burned out and had lost my passion for work. I was deeply unhappy and couldn't figure out how to make things better. So I walked away from my job as the CEO of Siemens Shared Services, a multimillion-dollar global company that provided administrative services for seventy thousand U.S.-based Siemens employees. To preserve my sanity, I exited a twenty-three-year career without looking back or ahead. With no plan B, I ran for the hills, or more accurately, the beach. I retreated to Nantucket Island off the coast of Massachusetts.

Within a matter of days of leaving my job, I went from running like a Tasmanian devil to sitting on a beach chair, hypnotized by the rolling waves, too tired to figure out what to do next. I expected to feel better immediately but soon realized that being at the beach every day would not make me happy.

After all, how do you abandon all the behaviors you need to successfully run a multimillion-dollar global business? You don't. Within four weeks, I had my first emotional crisis. A chance encounter at a local diner left me shaken. A man sitting next to me at the counter making friendly conversation asked me what I did. I replied: *"Nothing."* I used to be a CEO, but now my answer made me *feel* like nothing.

I knew that eventually I would have to go back to work, since I was only forty-six. But how could I avoid falling back into the same old patterns and behaviors that had made me miserable enough to drop out? I found answers with help from a new online friend, Mike Phelps, the Norton Simon professor and chair of the Molecular and Medical Pharmacology Department at UCLA, who became my teacher and guide to rediscovering what I loved in the work I thought I hated. Our email correspondence was a thoughtful dialogue about life lessons, beliefs, and values. Over time, I realized I was really writing to myself, not to Mike, and that I was slowly building a list of what I needed to be happy at work. With Mike's help, I figured out what was important to me and what I needed to sustain myself as a person. This made me feel renewed and restored—and ready to go back to work.

When I was ready, I was *eager* to go back to work. I rejoined Siemens after six months with a completely different attitude. I had changed my beliefs about work. A key realization was that I no longer needed to be the best; I was satisfied with *trying* my best, and this change in my thinking made all the difference. My priorities have never been clearer since.

Time off made this personal transformation possible for me, inducing a calmness that made me ready and able to listen to my own heart. I know that most people can't quit their jobs or take a sabbatical, and I don't recommend doing what I did in a down economy. But even a short period of time off from a high-stress job—whether you decide on your own or someone decides for you—can be a life-changing event for the better.

The collection of lessons in this book grew out of my email correspondence with Mike Phelps, as well as essays I wrote to remind myself about what is important to me about being happy at work. Many of them I posted as blogs on my website, **www.denicekronau.com**.

This is not your traditional self-help book, with step-by-step instructions on how to be happy at work. Being happy at work is a complex issue and, as such, has a complex answer. Maybe there is a formula or a structured process that can help you find that answer. But that's not what you'll find in this book. Instead, this book is organized in the way that I recovered from my burnout. It offers a series of linked observations that, taken together, showed me there were many, many things that made me happy at work. When I added them all up, I knew I could be happy at work again.

Here's what I know is true: only you can know what makes you happy at work. I also know that you already have many of the answers you seek; you only need to discover them. I believe these answers are like shells on the beach; take a mental walk through your own experiences with work, and you will find them at your feet. I hope that the observations I have shared here might become part of your own personal collection of shells that will help you regain your passion for work.

The Lessons

I Was Addicted to Work

Like all addictions, I had to admit I had a problem before I could get better. But when I ran away from my job, I did not realize my problem was one of addiction—I thought I was merely exhausted. And even worse, there was no one but me to blame. This was not an external force working its evil on me—the problem was within.

Three months into my sabbatical, my life in Nantucket had developed a rhythm that was soothing to my still-fragile state. I was spending a lot of time at the beach. The simple structure I had put in place in the first few weeks was like an old friend walking alongside me and holding my hand when I felt shaky. Meanwhile, Mike Phelps continued to send me emails, and I would respond.

Our emails were like little flashlights shining into the dark corners of my psyche. I was drawn to the insights Mike and I shared with each other because I was starting to understand that they were lighting the path to my future. I accepted that the reason I was so unhappy with work resided within me, and there was no external force pulling my strings like an evil puppet master. But why *didn't* I set boundaries for my behavior toward work? Why did work turn into something I was addicted to? A lesson from Mike helped me to understand this more clearly.

Mike was a Golden Gloves boxer in his youth. His boxing coach, Ira, once told him, "You must train and train until you are exhausted from it. Then, you must find it within you to train beyond this. In the beginning, you will win in the early rounds because you are a good fighter, but you must train to win in the late rounds, when you have nothing left but the will to win, because this is where you will face the very best and the winner will be decided."

I thought about the times in my work life when I felt I was training beyond exhaustion. I began to recognize the boundaries I lacked, the ones that could have kept me more balanced, preventing my addiction to work and its destructive impact on my day-to-day life. Here's an example of the insane choices I was making: I would fly sixteen hours from New York on a Saturday afternoon to attend a four-hour meeting in India on Monday, and fly back to New York immediately after the meeting.

From Mike's boxing analogy, I learned that pushing yourself is not the same as having no boundaries. I realized that I could still try very hard to achieve something important to me—to "win" at work—but that it did not have to become all consuming. While my behaviors up to this point had been those of an addict, I came to understand that it was the lack of boundaries that made my work so untenable. This insight was an essential element for restoring my energy for work.

QUESTIONS

1. Are there work behaviors that you are addicted to?

2. What are your boundaries? Do they keep you healthy and balanced?

Who You Are Is *Not* What You Do

When I started my sabbatical, I had certain expectations about how I would feel: a little sad, relieved, and uncertain about the future. I did not realize that not working would have a much bigger impact on me than no more paychecks. Unexpectedly, I went from being a CEO to being nothing—because if I wasn't working, then how could I explain who I was? I learned, the hard way, that I could only define myself by what I did for work. Realizing this was like getting punched in the stomach: it was swift, it was painful, and it took my breath away.

When I left my job and moved to Nantucket in the summer of 2005, I replaced my typical workday with a very different routine: wake up, check the weather, go to breakfast, and then go to the beach if the weather was nice.

My stomach punch came very unexpectedly. One morning I climbed onto the stool at the counter in my favorite breakfast place and ordered my usual: poached eggs, whole-wheat toast, and crispy bacon.

"Good morning," said the man next to me as I sat down.

"Good morning," I answered while nodding yes to the waitress, who poured me a cup of coffee.

"Beautiful day," my breakfast buddy added.

"Yes, it is. We're lucky this summer," I replied.

"You on vacation?" he asked.

"Nope, I live here."

"Jeez, that must be great. What do you do?"

"Nothing."

"Nothing?"

"Yup, nothing," I repeated.

"You don't work?"

"Nope."

"Wow, I would love to do nothing." At that point, he turned back to his wife and added politely, "Enjoy your breakfast."

"You too," I said.

I sat there, reeling. I felt ashamed that when asked what I did, the only thing I had to offer was "nothing." I didn't have the words to explain my situation, so I gave the easy answer. I had gone from being a CEO to being nothing because I had no job to define myself by. This answer made me *feel* like nothing.

That evening, I went for a drive on my Vespa scooter and let my mind wander. As the wind and bugs bounced off of my bare face and arms, I asked myself, "What if who I was *wasn't* what I did? How would people describe me? How would I describe myself?" I could always be my husband's wife or my parents' daughter or my brothers' sister, but this is not the Middle Ages. How did work become the *only* way I could define myself?

I spent a lot of time over the next days thinking about this and about how I wanted to answer this question in the future. I knew I did not want to answer "nothing" in conjunction with who I was ever again. Eventually I found the answers I was searching for, and when I went back to work six months later, I knew I would never define myself solely by my job title again.

I now describe who I am by what makes me happy. When I do this, I smile more and I am more me. I accept that what I do is a big part of who I am, not because of the title, but because of all of the factors that go into it—what I've achieved, how hard I've worked, the sacrifices I've made, and because the work itself reflects what I'm good at—and I'm OK with this. Now when I'm asked about my work, I no longer say, "I'm a CEO." Instead I say: "I lead a team that shares a mission, vision, and set of values, and because of this, I have the best job in our company." Compare the two statements. I am sure you know a lot more about me from the second one.

QUESTION   **1.** How do you describe who you are? Do you start with your job title?

Early Warning Signals to Help You Know If You Are Losing Your Passion for Work

How do you recognize when you are working too much and for the wrong reasons?

Who today truly keeps their perspective of what's normal or acceptable when it comes to work? Surviving the economic crisis of 2009 has pushed the limits of what is normal working behavior. The rules are changing, and more and more of us are working longer hours, giving up weekends, taking on impossible deadlines, doing work we hate—because of downsizing and fear of being laid off. And none of this is satisfying or rewarding; it's the work equivalent of the Bataan Death March.

Can you remember when you worked lots of hours because it was *fun*? Can you remember how it felt to finish a high-quality project on time, even if it meant long nights and weekends? You walked away from those moments knowing you had created something important, and most likely, you had done it together with your colleagues, so the shared experience of success was even more rewarding. In the months that followed, "Remember when we knocked that project out of the park?" would bring a smile to everyone's face and a renewed sense of energy for the task at hand.

This energy is the fuel for sustaining your passion for work. Without it, work is hard and definitely *not* fun. There's a series of questions you can ask yourself to see if you've emptied your work gas tank and are running on fumes:

1. How will you feel when this (project, task, trip, event) is over? Exhausted or energized?

2. If you didn't need the paycheck, would you still do this? And if you would still do it, would you truly enjoy doing it?

3. How many of your work hours, in percent of time, do you spend looking forward to the tasks at hand, or dreading them?
   a. Said another way, out of one hour, how many minutes are you happy?
   b. Is Sunday night the worst night of the week? Do you dread hearing the alarm clock ring on Monday morning?
   c. Do you find yourself settling for "good enough" when you used to take pride in the quality of your work?

4. Do you fantasize about getting sick or breaking your leg just to get some time off from work?

5. Do you get disproportionately angry when work intrudes on your time off? (Also known as "Why are those idiots calling me *now*?")

   a. Do your family and friends see this reaction and wonder what happened to the person they used to know?

6. Do things you used to take in stride now overwhelm you?

7. Do you negotiate with yourself about quitting—"If (your most painful thing) happens, then that's it, I'm leaving!"—and yet you never seem to pull the trigger?

8. Do you negotiate time not working with yourself? "I'll just watch the *Today Show* for ten more minutes, and then I'll work on emails." Have you regressed to when you were five years old and you wanted to watch TV *just five more minutes, Mom!*

Any one of these questions can be true at any given time for all of us. It's when two or three or four are true that it's clear that our passion for work has been replaced by a sense of obligation and even dread. Obligation is a bad coach; it never inspires us or gives us the energy we need to be happy at work.

QUESTION   1. Are more than three of these questions true for you?

Let's Talk About Being Happy at Work

Is it me, or is everyone a lot more interested in being happy at work than they have ever been before?

I talk about this topic a lot, as you would imagine. As soon as I do, I get an amazing response! We all know topics that nearly everyone can relate to. The weather springs to mind, and one of my favorites is travel horror stories. No matter who you talk to, everyone has their own: "Let me tell you about the time (*insert name here*) Airlines …"

I am finding that the topic of being happy at work triggers a more passionate response than even I would expect.

Why do you think this is? Is it more acceptable to want to be happy at work? When I started working nearly thirty years ago, no one ever talked about being happy at work. For the most part, work was hard, and we expected it to be—it was work!

I love where we are today. It's great that we've moved beyond seeing work as a chore, and I would offer it's been this way for many years. So why are we *talking* about it so much now? I have a simple answer: it's important to be happy at work, and because it's important, we should talk about it.

Talking kicks off new ideas. New ideas about how to be happy at work? Maybe. In any case, let's talk.

QUESTIONS
1. Do you think more people expect to be happy at work than they did before?

2. Do you talk about this with your colleagues?

Slow Down and Pace Yourself to Go the Distance

Sometimes amazing life lessons can come from surprising sources. I'd like to share the story of one such watershed moment in my own life, one that still helps keep me grounded at work twenty-five years later. I had forgotten all about this moment until I started writing to Mike Phelps.

I moved to New York for work in March 1985, and by that August, I had gained a lot of weight because I was eating pizza by the slice twice a day. (The culinary gods are groaning, but I am from upstate New York, where you have to buy the whole pizza; pizza by the slice is magic!) I decided to start running, for the obvious reasons. I joined the New York Road Runners Club, which held group runs twice a week in Central Park, meeting on the east side at Ninetieth Street. The leader of the group was a fifty-year-old man I'll call Mohammed; it was his responsibility to organize, by distance and pace, everyone who showed up to run. The main objective of the group run was to make sure all runners were safe; no runner ran in the park alone.

Mohammed, seeing I was new, asked me how far I was running.

"Two miles," I said. The farthest I had ever run in my life was a mile and a half, so two would be a stretch.

"The shortest distance is four miles; I'll run with you, and you will be fine," promised Mohammed.

I didn't object, but I was certain I would drop out after two miles. What was he going to do, drag me around the park? Within minutes of starting our run, I was panting and my head felt like an overripe tomato, ready to explode.

"Slow down," cautioned Mohammed. "No wonder you can only run two miles—you're running too fast."

We slowed down, and although my pulse was still in the upper triple digits, I was able to keep running. We crossed to the west side of the park, and I realized I would have to run the whole distance to get home. Tricked! I accepted my fate, but now I needed a distraction from my pain and misery, so I tried to get Mohammed to talk about himself.

"What do you do, Mohammed?" I panted.

"I am a night security man at a bank in Harlem, and I help people train for marathons," he said, clearly *not* out of breath.

"Wow," I said. "I could never run a marathon."

Mohammed softly replied, "Before today, you could never run four miles."

To this day, I can tell you exactly where we were in Central Park when Mohammed said this to me. You have to understand, I have never been athletic. When I was a kid and my mother told me to go outside and play, I took my book outside and hid. Mohammed's simple sentence transformed the way I thought about myself. He made me understand that what I am is up to me. And never, on a steamy night in August in New York City, did I imagine I would learn such an important lesson from such an unusual source.

That night, I floated home, which was good because in truth, I could hardly walk. From then on, I made one seemingly simple change: I ran more slowly, and as a result, I was able to run increasingly longer distances, surprising even myself. Four months later, I ran a 30k (18.6 mile) race in Central Park and, a year later, my first of four marathons. I went from a kid hiding outside to read my book to an adult who could run really, really slow marathons.

With a simple instruction—"slow down"—Mohammed significantly changed my thinking and my behavior. I was never going to run a competitive marathon—I changed my outlook, not my chubby, nonathletic body—but I didn't need to run competitively: just running a marathon was enough. I didn't have to win the race: I accepted that doing my personal best was more than enough because I was only doing this for me, not for anyone else.

These two lessons, "run slower" and "you are what you believe you are," were immediately relevant to my work. They eliminated barriers that I had imposed on myself. I tried new things at work I would not have tried before. I learned to pace myself and not work at a speed that added stress to the tasks at hand.

Mohammed was simply teaching me how to run longer distances, but in truth, his impact went well beyond the four-mile loop in Central Park. I believe we all have our Mohammeds who can take us by the hand and guide us through the marathons in both work and our lives.

I rediscovered these important lessons twenty-five years later as I was writing to Mike Phelps. Their memory popped up in my consciousness as I thought about work lessons I wanted to share with him. It was as if Mohammed had handed the baton to Mike, and I was glad to have a new coach running alongside me.

1. Can you remember a time when you learned a surprising lesson? Is it still true for you today?

2. Are you prepared to learn lessons from unexpected sources?

Picking Strawberries

Do you remember your first job? More specifically, do you remember when you first got paid to do something?

Mine was picking fruit.

I was ten years old, and my maternal grandmother, Stasia, had a strawberry patch in her yard. It seemed enormous to me at the time, but I'd guess it was about fifteen feet by thirty feet. This is a lot of strawberries.

"Do you want to make some money?" Stasia asked me when I was at her house one beautiful June morning. School was out for the year. Stasia lived two houses from ours, and my brothers and I were often visiting there.

"Sure! What do I have to do?" I replied.

"Take this and fill it with strawberries three times, and I will give you a quarter each time you fill it," she said, handing me the bottom drawer from her refrigerator. Seventy-five cents—I was going to be rich!

This drawer was the width and depth of the refrigerator, and if I had to estimate it now, I'd say it must have held at least twenty quarts of strawberries. *This* is a lot of strawberries.

But hey, I'm ten, and I have nothing else to do; school's out, and it's a beautiful summer morning, so I head out to strawberry patch and start picking.

I pick one. I eat one. They're delicious beyond description—so sweet, perfectly ripe.

I kept up my pattern for the next half hour.

Stasia stuck her head out of the back door. "How's it going out there?"

"Fine," I answered, looking at my progress. The drawer was about one-quarter full, and it had taken a half hour. I stopped eating them; I was pretty full by this time, and it was slowing me down. I realized that if I didn't pick up the pace, it was going to take me all day to get done.

A little over an hour later, I thought the drawer was full. It wasn't. There was still a two-inch gap between the level of the strawberries and the top of the drawer.

I went into the house, leaving my strawberries by the side of the patch, and told Stasia, "I'm done. Can I please have my quarter?" Stasia went out into the yard and came back into the house, empty-handed.

"You're not done. Get back out there."

"But Grammy, I think it's *enough* strawberries," I whined.

"No, it's not. You agreed to fill up the drawer, so go do it," she replied. I trudged back out to the strawberry patch and got back to work. I hated strawberries now.

In the end, it took me nearly all day to live up to my commitment—three refrigerator drawers filled to the top with strawberries. I had long breaks during the day—I was a kid, and I wasn't going to work for six or seven hours straight, nor would Stasia have expected me to.

From this experience, I learned stuff about working that I remember to this day. Work is hard. It can start out fun or seem easy, but to do a good job you have to do the work that's required and not just what you feel like doing. When you promise to do something, you have to finish it. Money is enticing, but remember—you're trading your time for it. I never expected to be picking strawberries all day. When you're the boss, be firm, but kind. Stasia didn't let me quit when I wanted to, but she did give me snacks and let me watch a little TV before I went back to work. When it's hard-earned, money has more value than its face value.

QUESTION 1. What lessons did you learn from your first jobs? Are they relevant to you today?

It's All in the Numbers

I found an article on **www.cbsnews.com** from January 10, 2010, titled "Survey: More Americans Unhappy at Work." It's worth reading.

It cites a recent Conference Board study that found that 55 percent of us are unhappy with our work, and 64 percent of workers under twenty-five are unhappy.

These are astonishing numbers. Think of it this way: if you're happy at work, then the odds are that the person sitting next to you is not.

This is worth fixing. I would like to sit in a room at work with twenty colleagues and have nineteen of them be happy to be there. OK, I'd even settle for eighteen. When one out of two people are unhappy, the whole tone of the office changes. Little irritants grow out of proportion to the incident. People are impatient, and no one listens. BlackBerries abound, as people would rather pay attention to their PDAs than to the people sitting next to them. Sound like any meetings you've attended recently?

One person can make a difference. You can make a difference. One person can change the tone of a meeting. I often use humor—probably sometimes inappropriately—to lighten the moment. This in and of itself doesn't make people happy at work, but I find it makes us all happy in the moment. And in that moment, 100 percent of the people are happy at work. It's a start.

QUESTIONS
1. Are you in the minority of people who are happy at work?
2. Does this surprise you?

What Is Light?

"What is light without the deepest of shadows?"
—Julia Glass, *More*, November 2010

I flew back to New York from Munich yesterday and read this quote by author Julia Glass in an article about surviving cancer titled "After the Big C."

It struck me profoundly. Here's why: I was recently reminded about the time in my work life when I felt I was living in the deepest of shadows.

Three weeks ago, I was at a meeting with forty people who are part of the same department as me. Among other topics, we were having a discussion about work-life balance, and I was asked to tell my story about dropping out in 2005 and coming back. They wanted to know about the warning signs: what indicators or behaviors should one recognize to prevent getting as burned out as I did?

I spoke for about five minutes, summarizing my crazy work life in 2005, and also explaining why I knew I would never work like that again. I explained that this is very personal; what was crazy for me might be someone else's "normal," and that the very best thing you can do is to be fully aware of what "crazy" and "normal" are for you. Whatever it might be: working late too many nights a week, working on the weekends, feeling stressed by deadlines—all of these examples only count if they mean something to you personally. Someone asked me if I had professional help during my time off, and I said I didn't, but I should have. I said I was so exhausted, I didn't even think to ask for help; I would definitely ask for professional help in the future.

I sat down after my little impromptu speech and hoped that what I said was at least a little helpful to my colleagues. In that moment, I thought about the contrast between my life now to my life then, and I was thankful that—as Julia Glass put it—I was no longer in the deepest of shadows.

I realize that overcoming work burnout is not the same as surviving cancer. But, if you feel you are in the "deepest of shadows," then who's to say how profoundly you can be affected by feeling overwhelmed with work?

A surprising thing has happened: several colleagues have come up to me since our meeting and thanked me for my comments. First, they were surprised I was so open about what happened, and that I admitted

I handled it badly—as we all know, walking away from work is hardly a constructive action. And, to a person, they said they were inspired to take action because they themselves were feeling frustrated and unsure about how to act. They were encouraged to learn that both the problems and answers were personal: on some level, each of them felt isolated and worried that their feelings were not normal. My story showed them that anyone—at any level—could be worried and afraid, and with the right help, get to a better, happier place.

QUESTIONS

1. Do you avoid thinking about unhappiness at work because you believe it's not normal?

2. If you were happily returning to work, what do you think would be your motivation to return?

Happy and Sad

I flew from New York to Boston on December 18, 2009. Because I travel so much for work, I am at the highest level of most airline mileage programs, so I often get better seats (aisle, exit row) or upgraded to first class, as happened this time. As I waited for my flight, I noticed several Army folks in uniform also in the waiting room. A thought popped into my head: "Give your seat to one of these guys."

"I have a favor to ask you," I said to the flight attendant as I boarded the plane. The flight attendant looked at me, wondering what in the world I was going to ask for, as I was already sitting in first class. I continued, "I want to give my seat to one of the servicemen who is about to get on the plane."

She looked surprised. "You don't have to do that," she said. "We are happy to move the folks up if there are empty seats. You don't have to give up yours."

I persisted. "If you don't have enough seats, I will give up mine." In truth, this was a small thing to do, and if I didn't travel for work as much as I do, I would have probably not been so inclined to give up my first-class seat to someone else.

The plane boarded, and sure enough, first class was nearly full, with only one empty seat. Five servicemen got on the plane. The flight attendant came to me. "We don't have enough places for all of them, but if you're still willing, we can move up two." She went to economy and brought back two of the folks. The first one sat in the empty seat, and I got up out of mine, to the surprise of the soldier standing in the aisle.

"Thank you, ma'am!"

"Enjoy the ride," I replied as I moved to economy. I sat in an empty seat and settled in for the short flight to Boston, kind of wishing that it was a longer flight so that the soldier could enjoy first class longer. Even though it was a small gesture, I felt very good that I could do something nice for one of our soldiers.

A little later in the flight, another flight attendant was serving drinks and quietly said to me, "You will be the topic of our dinner conversation tonight. Each night, I try to teach my seventeen-year-old son a lesson about life and people. You will be the subject of tonight's lesson, about how your small gesture made a difference in a young man's life." My cheeks turned red, and I felt slightly embarrassed—I felt like I was getting way too much attention for this.

As I share this with you, I am happy and sad. Happy to have had this feel-good moment, and sad too, because how sad is it that something so small—giving up a first-class seat on a forty-minute flight—should be something to remark on, and not just be part of our daily routine? Are we all getting so hardened by the current times that a small, truly insignificant gesture becomes more than it is?

QUESTIONS
1. Can you remember a time when a small gesture had a big impact on you?

2. When a thought of kindness spontaneously pops into your head, do you act on it?

We All Want to Get an A

I have a friend, Drew, who has autism. He's nearly twenty-two years old and has graduated from school. Drew has had many part-time jobs in the last couple of years, and he likes going to work.

He recently started a new job bagging groceries at a grocery store near his home. Drew is a funny, charming person. Let me give you an example: when I heard about his new job, I bought him a pen as a congratulations-on-your-new-job present. I bought the pen in Germany, and when I sent the pen to Drew I explained that the pen came from Germany. Drew sent me a thank-you note, and he had drawn a picture of a dog on the note. It was cute. I said thank you for the picture of my dog, and Drew's response was, "It's a German shepherd because the pen came from Germany!"

This job was different from the jobs Drew had in the past; he did not have a buddy at work, and while everyone at the store was very kind to him, there wasn't one person looking out for him. Drew was learning how to bag groceries, and he did a good job, but he was slower than a more experienced person. Some of the customers did not have a lot of patience. We all know the feeling—going to the grocery store is a chore, and we just want to get in and out as quickly as possible.

Drew had worked at the store for a week when he got his first paycheck. His mother shared this story with me, and I would like to share it with all of you because it really struck a chord with me.

Drew brought home his first paycheck, and the paystub was on the kitchen table.

"Mom," Drew said, "did I get an A?"

His mother was confused. What was Drew talking about?

"My report card," he persisted. "Did I get an A at work?"

"Drew, I don't know what you're talking about. Please show me."

Drew picked up his paystub and handed it to his mother. "Here, look at this. It's my report card from work. Tell me if I got an A."

Drew's mother smiled at the new interpretation of a paystub and said, "Yes, Drew, you got an A."

"Good," said Drew, who then happily went off to his room.

Because of Drew's special needs, he will never go through a normal performance review like most folks in corporate America. No one is going to set objectives, measure outcomes, or rate his performance once or twice a year. And yet Drew was very keen to know if he got an A at work. In his own way, Drew's a high achiever, as he does not want to settle for less than the best.

I loved this story because it brought me back to first principles: we all want an A at work. True, performance management at work is much more complicated than our school report cards, but the desire is the same. It also reminded me that surprising lessons can come from anywhere if we're open to hearing them.

QUESTIONS

1. What motivates you at work?

2. Do you want to get an A?

Tunnel Vision

Did you know cupcakes are the new brownies?

I took Amtrak from Boston to New York on January 2, 2010, and sat next to a very engaging young man. Shortly after the train left South Station, my seatmate and I started chatting. One topic led to another, and we were soon discussing desserts (doesn't everyone?), and he told me about the cupcake breakthrough. How did I miss this? I *love* cupcakes!

As it was a playful conversation; we bounced around to many different topics, and the "What do you do?" question did not come up for several minutes. When we started talking, I had my PC open, and I was working on my book. He asked if I was a writer, and I said "aspiring," and that I was also a chief financial officer.

Why am I telling you this? In the "olden days," I would have had my laptop open and been furiously attacking the mountain of work emails that piled up day after day. C'mon—aren't emails the work version of Whack-A-Mole, minus the fun? I most likely would have never engaged in a conversation in the first place. If I did speak to a stranger, I would always bring up my job very early in the conversation—like most folks, this was one of the defining elements of who I was. This time, I started talking about what I loved—writing and desserts!

When I was working like a crazy person, I would get very absorbed by my world and often find myself narrowing my experiences to only those related to work. Even if you're wildly in love with your job, when work is all you think about, then you miss the momentous occasions in your life—like when cupcakes overtake brownies in the dessert hierarchy! (OK, maybe this is only a momentous occasion in *my* life.)

QUESTIONS

1. When you meet someone new, how long does it take before you ask: "What do you do?" or "Where do you work?"

2. In social situations, what percentage of your time do you spend talking about work?

Thirty Years from Now, What Difference Will It Make?

From the age of sixteen until twenty, I worked part-time at our family dentist, Dr. Dunn. My aunt Chris was his office manager, and I was his assistant.

My responsibilities included cleaning the treatment rooms between patients, greeting patients, developing X-rays, and recording the treatment on the patients' files—all normal assistant duties.

Dr. Dunn was an interesting person. He had been a fighter pilot in World War II and had a charismatic, strong personality. To be honest, I was a little bit afraid of him. He would regale each patient with his story of the day, be it about his kids, his car, or his golf score. I heard each of these stories up to ten times a day, as I would stand patiently and silently in the treatment room, waiting for an instruction. While these were stories about his everyday life, somehow each of his stories had a moral, and he would end almost every one with: "Tell me, Miss Kronau, thirty years from now, what difference will this make?"

Every time he did this, I would stutter my reply, as I was unsure of how to respond. Did he want me to say that I thought the issue was unimportant? That in thirty years we will have all long forgotten what this conversation was about? Remember, I'm sixteen. Dr. Dunn was in his fifties, and pretty intimidating. I don't remember my answers; I only remember that I felt flustered and very unsure of myself.

Why am I sharing this with you? And what does it have to do with being happy at work?

I realized many, many years after working for Dr. Dunn that his question taught me how to evaluate what is happening in the moment in the context of how important it was to me. Will whatever it is really matter to me in thirty years? In five years? Next week? This question has helped me keep things in perspective when, in the heat of the moment, it seems like the issue in front of me is overwhelming. Now, when I find myself in such a situation, I can hear Dr. Dunn's voice play in my head: "Miss Kronau, thirty years from now …" While I hated his comment when I was sixteen, today it takes a lot of pressure off of tense moments at work. This is always helpful.

It was an unexpected lesson for me, and I am sure all of you have similar lessons from your early work experiences.

Dr. Dunn, more than thirty years later, I can honestly say that learning this from you made a significant difference to me.

QUESTIONS

1. Would this question help you keep things in perspective?

2. What if you shortened the time frame? Thirty weeks from now? Thirty days from now?

"If I Only Had Just One More Day ..."

If I had five cents for every time I said this, I would be writing this from my yacht in the Caribbean!

One of the best gifts I ever gave myself was to stop wishing for more time. Since I've done this, I am much happier in general, not just at work. "If I only had one more hour to work on … (fill in the blank—presentation, spreadsheet, preparing for a meeting)." I used to hate deadlines. Not because I couldn't live by them, but because it meant whatever I was working on had a hard stop, and I knew if I had just *a little more time*, I could make it better. Frankly, all this did was make me very frustrated and unhappy.

None of us can manufacture time.

During my sabbatical, I thought about all of the things that made me happy and unhappy at work. I knew if I was to be happy at work again, I had to do more of the stuff that made me happy and try to minimize the stuff that made me miserable—such as cursing the ticking clock!

I decided to look at time as a finite resource like any other limited resource and not as something to keep wishing for. Wishes are for shooting stars and blowing out the candles on your birthday cake, not for getting through my workday. I now look at each deadline and consciously decide how much time I will allot it. Preparing for a meeting—one hour. Writing a presentation—three hours. Talkin' to my peeps—four hours. For me, this has been unbelievably liberating. I get it wrong; sometimes my estimates are poor. I trade. I trade time on task A for time on activity B. And sometimes I trade free time for task A, especially if it's something that gives me a lot of personal satisfaction.

I still don't get it right all the time, and I find myself slipping back into old habits. I expect I will keep practicing this new behavior until I die!

QUESTION 1. Do you actively manage your time, or do you curse the clock?

Creature Comfort

Can I please rant for a minute?

When did business conferences become endless twelve- to fourteen-hour marathons? This is when I am most *unhappy* at work.

My attention span gets shorter and shorter as conferences get longer. Skip lunch, skip breaks, serve bad coffee—you would have a better chance of me dancing the polka instead of paying attention. The only contribution I'm willing to make in these circumstances is to create a doll of the conference organizer and start sticking pins in it.

I don't understand the logic of these types of events. Does anyone really think we get more done if we hold people hostage in a meeting room for more than four hours?

When I plan a meeting or a conference, I cater to my ability to sit still, which is for about an hour at a time. I also don't think starting early improves any event. When I organize a meeting, I tell the attendees, "We start at 9 AM. If it's critically urgent to do so, we can start at 8 AM. Anything before 8 AM is yesterday, so it's not going to happen."

I organize excellent snacks, a decent lunch break (amount of time + food), and finish with at least a one-hour gap between the end of the day's topics and the evening event. If it's a multi-day event, I always organize something fun for one of the evenings—it's just lazy to simply make a restaurant reservation. Bowling, anyone? I *will* break one hundred at some point ...

I go to more and more conferences and meetings where simple creature comfort is completely disregarded. Thirty people in a room for twenty, no natural light all day, temperature too hot or too cold: all of these things sound petty and childish to even complain about, but they do impact the quality of the event. I'm sure you agree that when people are cranky, the desired outcome is never as good. Tempers get short—well, I know mine does—and the ability to collaborate is lost.

Here's all I ask: if you want me at your meeting, *please* let me organize it—I'll bring the cupcakes! See you at 9 AM ...

QUESTIONS

1. How long can you pay attention in a meeting?

2. Think about a great meeting you attended recently. What was great about it?

Loyalty and Friendship at Work

Loyalty and friendship do not trump being true to your values.

Some of my closest friends are ones I made at work. As we all know, we spend more time with these folks than with most of the friends we have outside of work. We have shared experiences, a shared language, and a shared context—all of which contribute to very strong friendships.

This is both good and bad.

Good is clear. Why would I say it's bad? Recently I faced a situation where I had to choose between being loyal to my friend and doing what I thought was right, which would hurt my friend and jeopardize our friendship. It was purely political and would have no negative impact on the company. C'mon—the direction is clear when you know your actions will harm the company—as Nancy Reagan said, "Just say no!"

To take the action I thought was right, my friend would lose, and one of his political rivals would win—and my action would be the catalyst that would bring all of this out into the open. I contemplated doing nothing, but unfortunately this was not an option. I admit it: sometimes I'm a chicken!

I had a few days to consider what I wanted to do before I had to act. From the outside, I am sure it seems black-and-white—do what's right! But I am fiercely loyal to my friend. This friend has stood by me many times when work was nearly unbearable and had helped me in more ways than I could possibly cover in a short essay. I *hated* the thought of causing my friend any pain or trouble.

After three sleepless nights, I had to step outside of the moment and virtually go back to my favorite beach on Nantucket. I listened to wave sounds on my iPod. The answer slowly formed in my brain, like the tide coming in: do what I think is right. If my friend was the person I thought he was, he would not want me to do anything else. He would not ask me to swap my personal integrity for friendship. Loyalty to your friends does not come before loyalty to your own values and beliefs.

How did it turn out? Without compromising the situation, I was able to give my friend a heads-up before it happened, and this helped. I was definitely not his favorite person for a few days. I stayed true to my values, and today our friendship is back to normal. All friendships go through highs and lows, and the ones at work are no different.

1. Have you been in a similar situation? How did it turn out?

2. Are some of your closest friends people you work with?

My In-box Is Always Full

My email in-box is always full. How about yours?

In the last five years, I have gotten my in-box down to four emails for about three hours. For me, this is similar to being on a diet. I can tell you the exact number of *hours* I could wear size two jeans.

I average four hundred to five hundred emails in my in-box at any one time. Sometimes I get a burst of energy, and I clear out a couple hundred, but, like rabbits, they multiply, and I'm right back to north of four hundred.

I have a few simple rules about email:

- Each message stays in my in-box until I've read it and determined if I need to do something with it.

- It gets electronically filed only when I no longer need to touch it again.

- The emails I like the best are the ones I can answer immediately.

Do you have a hierarchical filing system for your emails? I used to. I can't remember where I filed the stupid thing anymore. It goes like this: did I file it under the organization it came from, or under the person's name, or according to the topic? I know people who will create copies and file one email in three places. Yikes. I can never remember the logic of my filing system, so I've simplified it: unread, better known as my in-box, or read, filed in the folder cleverly named "Read emails." Dazzling.

This is another aspect to my new approach to work: I don't let emails nag or haunt me. They used to; I would drown in email quicksand every Sunday afternoon. I would dive in, send out hundreds, and cause email misery for all of my team because even though I said they could ignore them until Monday, they would all, to a person, answer them on Sunday. This did not make them or me happy.

I now ignore the email siren song. If I want to be *unhappy* at work, I just listen for Lorelei's singing and am drawn onto the rocks of my in-box. I like that I am the captain of my email ship, and I only navigate the waters that keep me on an even keel.

What's your secret to keeping your sanity about email? I'd love to hear it. Send me an email at **denice@denicekronau.com**. I promise: I will read it!

1. Similar to my email in-box, is there one activity at work that you can never seem to get ahead of?

2. Can you devise a strategy that turns it from work quicksand into a day at the beach?

Even the Best People Need Encouragement

A few years ago I was on a flight from Bangalore to New York, traveling with Fred, our company's chief financial officer. Fred is one of the best people I have ever worked with. He is a talented and dedicated leader, and I was lucky to have him as my partner. But on that flight, Fred was discouraged and exhausted from all our recent hard work and because he believed that our team was not 100 percent with us and that we were not making enough progress. I empathized with his frustration, but I did not share his point of view. I realized that I had to help Fred. As he slept beside me in the window seat, I wrote six presentation charts about what it meant to be a leader in our company. I highlighted our values as a company and my personal values as a leader. When Fred woke, I showed him my charts and told him I knew that—together with the rest of our team—we could achieve amazing things. He smiled, and I saw him regain his spark.

The qualities that enable top-notch people to perform at their best can also mask the fact that they are also human beings and that they need encouraging, too. The folks who perform at extraordinary levels, day after day, always appear to be so self-sufficient, as if they're running on Energizer Bunny batteries. It did not occur to me, until that moment, that Fred might need encouragement from me. Why didn't I know this? Didn't I also need to have people recognize my efforts? Yes, I did. We all do.

This was a great wake-up call for me, and I now make a conscious effort to recognize the extraordinary performance from the folks I trust and rely on and to *never* take them for granted.

QUESTIONS
1. Who among your closest colleagues do you unwittingly take for granted?

2. Do you make a conscious effort to recognize and thank the colleagues who quietly, yet heroically, perform day after day?

A Day Off Means *Off*

I was on Nantucket recently, very happy to have a week off of work. Being happy at work does not equal being happy to work all of the time.

During this week, Nantucket was like a beautifully wrapped present with my name on it. The weather was glorious: blue skies, light breezes, and temperatures in the sixties. I was at the beach every day.

I have had to learn how to not work on my days off. Before my sabbatical, I would often take days off and find myself working remotely instead of not working at all. I'm sure you have had the same experience—just checking emails quickly, hopping on a brief call—whatever it is you think you can squeeze in and still be able to call the day a day off.

The problem for me is that whatever I did was not really quick; it always took more time than I had expected. And often, the topic would ricochet in my brain like a ball in a pinball machine. It was hard to relax when this was the background noise.

So what do I do differently now? If I only take one day off, I shut off my BlackBerry for the entire day. I have colleagues who can look after whatever is urgent, and most things can wait a day or two. If something has a strict deadline, then the same colleagues can reach me on my personal BlackBerry. I only give this number to a very select few folks. With my current responsibilities, it's difficult for me to be completely unreachable, so I compromise and limit the folks who can reach me. This works really well.

What happens when I take a week or two off from work?

It's been years since I've had a job that I could completely shut off for a week. I accept that I will need to check in periodically and keep the urgent stuff moving. I do this by email. Here's what a week off looks like: I check emails Tuesday morning, Wednesday evening, and Friday morning for anything that can be done only by me. *Everything else waits.* It's tempting—I see an email that I could forward to someone quickly, and get it out of my in-box—and as soon as I do this, there are twenty more just like it. Remember, emails breed like rabbits! If I am disciplined and stick to this process, I never work more than three hours on a week off. There's only been one time when it took longer than I had planned. There's another advantage of this system: I also quiet my inner nag that insidiously suggests, "Do work, check email, do work, check email"—stopping the pinball in my head before it starts bouncing around.

As I write this, it sounds easy. I found it really hard to learn. The best way I can reinforce this habit is for me to be somewhere I love on my days off—such as Nantucket—or to be with people I love, doing something fun. This is my carrot for good behavior, because I find working on a day off is always a stick!

QUESTIONS

1. When you take time off, are you really off? Or are you just working remotely?

2. Can you establish a routine for days off that meets your work obligations and your need to have a break?

Verbal Stop Signs: "No" and "But"

I recently attended some meetings at which a lot of new ideas were discussed. Some of them were pretty wild—definitely out-of-the-box ideas. Nearly all of the participants reacted very negatively to the new ideas and spent a lot of time explaining why they wouldn't work. It was like a rugby scrum of naysayers piling on the poor little new ideas.

Why do we do this? Is it a defense mechanism? New + I don't understand = it must be bad.

I've found it's worthwhile to *not* react negatively to new ideas. I've trained myself to hear something new and ask: "What would happen if it was successful? Would things be better?" If I answer yes to either question, I then ask myself, "What do I need to do to make this new idea work?"

And don't get me started on "but." We have a rule at our team meetings: no one is allowed to use the word "but." Using "but" is a sneaky way of disagreeing with someone without being open about it.

"I really like your idea, but help me understand how it will work." Translation: I think your idea has no chance of working.

"We can try it your way, but I think the way we always do it is also effective." Translation: We're not changing the way we do things.

"That's a fabulous sweater, but the color is so unusual." Translation: Did you look in the mirror before you left your house?

"No" and "but"—take them out of your vocabulary at work, and I think you will find it's much easier to get things done. I found it really hard to do this, and I catch myself trying to say "but" about twenty times a day. I swap "and" for "but," and this completely changes the tone of the discussion.

"I really like your idea, *and* please help me understand how it will work." Translation: I want to know more about what you're suggesting.

"We can try it your way, *and* I think the way we always do it is also effective." Translation: We'll give your idea a try with the safety net of what works today.

"That's a fabulous sweater, *and* the color is so unusual." Translation: I'll get you one for your birthday! (OK, maybe *and* doesn't work every time!)

This makes the atmosphere at work more open and the interaction with your colleagues more constructive. No? I could be wrong, but …

QUESTIONS

1. Do you use "but" a lot?

2. What would happen if you eliminated it from your vocabulary?

Striking a Balance

I speak at management classes in our company as often as my schedule permits. The most frequently asked question is: "How do you balance your work life and your personal life?" The person who asks always has a hopeful look on his face—as if I might have the secret of working a sane amount of hours—and I disappoint him every time.

I answer: "Are you are asking me if I keep my work hours in a nearly equal proportion to my hours outside of work? If this is your question, then no, I don't. I consciously choose to spend a lot of hours working, and my recent jobs are very demanding and time-consuming."

Here's the key point: I *consciously choose* to work the hours I work. This is why it's essential for me to be happy at work.

The proportion of my week that I allocate to work is high—there are 168 hours in a week, and I will typically work sixty to seventy hours (if you include time spent traveling). I try to sleep eight hours a day (key word = "try"), so there's another fifty-six hours. During the week, a typical workday will start at 8 AM and usually ends around 9 PM.

One hundred sixty-eight hours in a week minus fifty-six hours of sleep minus seventy working hours equals forty-two hours awake and not working, or 25 percent of my week.

Now subtract time for normal maintenance that has to get done: grocery shopping, laundry, and paying bills… well, the time left over for family and fun is probably about 10–15 percent of my week.

How do we like the math so far? This formula works for me. But everyone has to do his or her own math. I am sure folks with children would have 0 percent unplanned time!

In an odd way, it's good news. When you are really clear about how much time you are willing to invest in work and where the trade-offs come from, then being happy is a natural outcome.

QUESTIONS

1. Create your own equation. How much time per week do you have available for fun?

2. Are the proportions between work, sleep, maintenance, and fun what you expected?

Lesson from an In-flight Movie: Do Better

I flew from Munich to New York recently, and during the flight I watched *Invictus*, the movie about Nelson Mandela's presidency and the 1995 rugby World Cup in South Africa.

In the movie, Morgan Freeman, playing Nelson Mandela, tells the story about attending the 1992 Olympics in Barcelona. He said that they played a song in honor of him and South Africa, and when he heard this song, he was very proud to be South African. He said it inspired him to go home to South Africa and "do better."

I know that when I strive to do better—at whatever I'm working on—I am happier.

For example, I am inspired to do better when I am working together with people I value and respect. It motivates me to go the extra mile, even if I'm tired or think I have nothing more left to give.

What (or who) motivates you to do better? And I would also ask you this: whom do *you* inspire to do better?

In my life, I have had three extraordinary bosses. The one trait that they had in common was that every time I met with each of them, I left the meeting wanting to do better. We would review open topics and, often, troubling challenges and problems. Our meetings were focused on the tasks in front of us. They never explicitly said anything motivating; however, somehow it snuck up on me. I always left the room wanting to do better.

We often think of motivation and inspiration as playing a role in big, important events—such as Nelson Mandela's inspiring leadership in bringing an end to apartheid in South Africa. But I also think you can make these topics personal; you bring them into your day-to-day work life by trying to do better every day and by inspiring those around you to do better, too.

QUESTIONS
1. What or who inspires you to do better?
2. Who do you inspire?

Finding Common Ground

I travel around the world for my work, working with people from more than forty countries. I am often asked: "How can we build a common culture when we are all different people from such different countries?" Sometimes, the question is directed to me personally: "Denice, how will you ensure that our organization has a common culture?"

I always respond with a question: "Did you come to work today hoping you will be mediocre?" On your way in to work, did you say to yourself, "I hope I can be *really* average today?" I am sure you would answer no to both. I am also very sure that you came into the office today hoping to do your best. Maybe you couldn't; maybe something came up that kept you from doing your best—we all have days when our best is not in reach. But you did not intend to be average or mediocre.

This is our common culture. Wherever I work, I strive to recreate this culture, as I personally find it very nourishing and rewarding. As human beings, we aspire to do our best. This is a great common ground to share, and it's essential for being happy at work.

QUESTIONS

1. Besides the actual work, what do you have in common with your colleagues?

2. Does this make you happy at work?

The Moments That Make a Life

This lesson has nothing to do with being happy at work. It's about being happy in life.

One of my closest friends, Willy, recently died unexpectedly in his sleep.

There are lots of things written about death, and I am hardly going to add anything original to the existing body of work.

I can explain my relationship with Willy like this: he was family I picked for myself. Willy and I were the spouses of graduate school classmates: my husband, Michael, and his wife, Trudy. Michael and Trudy are very good friends, and this friendship was extended to Willy and me.

I moved to Hoboken, New Jersey, in 2002, and Trudy and Willy lived nearby. From the start, we spent so much time together—Costco, movies, dinners, Short Hills Mall—you name it. We were together nearly every weekend.

Then, in 2004, I gave up my apartment in Hoboken to live in Nantucket. As I traveled nearly 60 percent of the time, this is not as illogical as it sounds. I was only in my official office in Iselin, New Jersey, four to five days a month. I needed a place to stay when I was in the office, so I would stay with Trudy and Willy. They had a relatively small apartment, and I am quite sure if the situation was reversed I would not have been as generous about sharing my limited space with them five days or so a month. Not only did they let me sleep there, they treated me like a treasured guest: feeding me fabulous dinners, letting me watch my favorite TV shows, and generally taking good care of me.

This was a very hard time for me. Work was getting harder and harder, and I was trying to decide if I should stay or go. I can imagine that I was not so easy to live with this during this time, and yet I can't remember Trudy and Willy being anything but welcoming each time I showed up at their house. In hindsight, I realize that Willy was a part of the daily fabric of my life that I took for granted.

On the days I stayed with them, I would arrive at their apartment and Trudy would be in the kitchen, fixing some fabulous dinner after working a long day (do I sound guilty enough?), and Willy would be tinkering with something on one of his many computers. At this time, there was always some drama in my workday that was all-consuming, and I would burst through the door, dispense with the niceties, and launch into whatever it was—really, I was the poster child for "it's all about me."

"Dee, tell me what's going on," Willy would say as he put down his computer to listen to me.

"This (insert drama) is making me crazy," I would say, frustrated by the day's events. "I just don't know what to do or how I'm going to get through it."

"Do you have to do anything this very minute?" Willy asked. "Can you watch some TV and enjoy your dinner?"

As simple as this sounds, his comments would bring me back from drama-land, and I would immediately relax. He was right: there was never anything that had to be done *right this minute*. His sentence reminded me to take a breath, a concept I had completely lost sight of.

Willy's death has left such a hole in so many lives. I feel absolutely selfish when I think about how much I will miss him, realizing that my loss is tiny compared to his family's. For everyone who loved him and was loved by him, Willy was the safe dock in a protected harbor. His friendship gave each of us a place to sail to when the seas of life got too stormy.

His family and friends have no choice but to carry on captaining our little ships without Willy. But he taught us well. I know that people like Willy, who love unconditionally, give us the greatest gifts of all: a place where we're protected, and the courage to find our own way in the world.

QUESTION   **1.** Is being unhappy at work keeping you from being happy in life?

How Early Is Too Early?

Does anything *really* good happen before 9 AM?

I am firmly convinced it doesn't.

I think talking before noon is unnecessary. I am perfectly fine with *other* people talking before noon; I just pray they don't want a response from me.

We all have our own rhythms when certain things click and others don't. I am my most intellectually creative between 5 and 9 AM. After 9 AM, I have to work harder at it. When I have to think big thoughts, I will set my alarm to get up early: to write or draw or think. But not to talk; I can't tell anyone about my revelations until late morning.

I accept that there are obligations at work that do not always fit nicely into one's own personal rhythms. Adapting to our environment makes life simpler and easier, but maybe not happier. Here's what I do: I try to find ways to compromise and be happy at the same time. I follow the schedule that business normally runs on—it would be really inefficient if there were no meetings before noon—and when it's up to me, I will schedule all talking events to start later than 11 AM.

If you're the person who is chatty and raring to go at 7 AM, good for you. Please, just don't sit next to me.

QUESTIONS
1. Does anything good happen before 9 AM?
2. Do you know what works best for your biological clock?

Giving and Taking Credit

In my job, I often host events—meetings, discussion groups, and the like. Sometimes I invite folks to events that are more social in nature, like a breakfast or cocktail party.

I recently invited a group of senior women in our company to a cocktail party. They were all attending another meeting, and the idea behind the cocktail party was to hold a networking event to take advantage of their presence at the bigger event.

It was so much fun! This was the first time this group had met each other, and the energy in the room was spectacular. At one point, I stood to the side and watched the participants talk, laugh, and connect with each other—I was happy we organized it. At the end, each attendee thanked me, genuinely pleased to have been invited.

"Denice, this is *such* a great idea. Thank you so much for the invitation," said one participant.

"You're welcome," I replied. "But it wasn't my idea. It was Rosa's." I couldn't take the credit for this—it would have made me feel terrible. I was getting all the thanks just because I sent out the invitation.

Rosa asked me later why I gave her the credit for the idea; she was really OK with me taking the credit for it. And I understand this—very often it's important that the *team* takes the credit for something, not one person on the team. This wasn't one of those moments; she deserved the credit.

During our work life, we are so often in this position—when a success is attributed to one person, but in fact it may belong to another. This makes me *unhappy* at work. Not just because it's unfair, though it is. It makes me unhappy because you miss something really special when you don't give credit where it is due. And it also causes mistrust between colleagues—how much can you trust someone who deliberately takes credit for something you've done?

Rosa was slightly embarrassed as I kept telling everyone who thanked me that it was her idea. I thought about her reaction later, and I understood it. Being part of a team is drummed into us; it feels awkward or uncomfortable to take sole credit for something.

But if you're the person who deserves the credit, my advice is: take it. You earned it. Be proud that you've done something that's worth getting the credit for—and when it's your turn to give credit to someone else, remember how good it feels to be recognized for doing something well. It also strengthens the bonds of the team when you support each other in this way. This is a great way to be happy at work!

QUESTIONS

1. Do you give credit where it's due?

2. Are you reluctant to take credit?

The Opposite of Talking...

Is *not* "waiting to talk."

When did we all stop being able to listen? When did what we have to say become so urgent that we have to blurt it out *right this minute*, even if someone else is talking?

This is my number one pet peeve, and, I would offer, one of the biggest single contributors to what makes work hard and, at times, frustrating. If nobody's listening, then so much time is wasted because we miss potentially acting on good ideas that go unheard.

Yes, I concede that there are people who talk much longer than they should. But most people know how to say what they have to say and give the next person his or her turn. Skilled moderators or conversation partners know how to gracefully interrupt those long-winded folks. Did we lose the skill of how to listen politely?

There are classes and seminars about listening. Listening well is not easy; you have to quiet your own inner voice to really listen to someone else. It takes focus, and you have to put energy into it. Just think about how hard it is to listen to anyone when you're tired.

But do we really need to attend a class before we can get better at this? Or can we just think back to what we learned in kindergarten?

- Everyone gets a turn
- We all have to share

And another of my pet peeves:

- Please use your indoor voice

Here's what I suggest: the next time you're in a meeting and feeling frustrated, pay attention to what's happening. I would bet that there is a lot of talking and very little listening. I have learned to stop it in a way that makes my point and is funny at the same time. I ask, "Can someone tell me what is the opposite of talking?" This usually causes a confused look on most people's faces—is this a trick question? Finally, a brave soul suggests, "Listening." "Wow," I reply. "Watching us today, I thought the opposite of talking was waiting to talk." This usually gets a laugh, and for the rest of the meeting, people try to do better at listening.

It may not be sustainable, but it's a good start.

QUESTIONS

1. At work, do you listen, or are you waiting to talk?

2. Think about a meeting or discussion when you were very frustrated and unhappy. Was it because people weren't listening to you?

Throw It Out

I am moving house again. I've lost count of how many times I've moved: it's well over twenty.

I like to throw things away when I move. I *really* like to throw my husband Michael's things away. Here's why: the first time we moved together, Michael did not want to throw *anything* away.

It was a Saturday afternoon, and I was packing up the kitchen.

"What's this?" I asked Michael, holding up a small, twisted piece of metal that I found on the windowsill.

He looked up from the newspaper and replied, "No idea."

"Did it break off of something?" I persisted.

"I don't know," he answered.

"I'm going to throw it out."

"No!"

The small, twisted piece of metal went into the box.

Michael's ability to influence my overarching need to purge was severely diminished by this exchange. If I don't know what it is and why I need it, why would I think it's worth keeping? And even worse, I will hate finding a new place for it in the future.

Stuff at work that makes me unhappy is the same. Too often, we find a place for something that's broken, or doesn't fit anymore. I think we believe that if we always had it, then we must need it—whatever it is. I have a simple answer: throw it out, and move on.

Yes, this is one of my secrets about how to be happy at work: pretend you're moving house and you're only taking what you need and love with you to the new house (or job). Just don't ask me about my blue jeans from high school …

QUESTION   1. How much do you carry around that you could really throw out?

Gratitude

I was recently on Nantucket, and I picked up a copy of Cary Hazlegrove's new book, *Nantucket*.

Cary is a well-known, accomplished photographer, and she takes wonderful, beautiful photos of Nantucket. When I try to explain to someone what Nantucket is like, I give the person one of Cary's books. She captures the essence of the island in two dimensions. Her photos evoke memories that engage all five senses.

And it's not just the photos that describe Nantucket, but also the words. In *Nantucket*, there's a quote from Karen Borchert that I fell in love with:

"Gratitude accumulates here."

I know this is true. Every time I am on the island, I am so grateful to be there. I feel this gratitude deep in my stomach. It's a little voice that says: "You work very hard. You travel a lot. You make trade-offs to do the job that you do. And once in awhile, you can come home to Nantucket. The trade-offs are worth it."

This is also true: we all have our own "Nantuckets" that we are grateful for. For me, it's a place. For many folks, it's taking care of their families. It's never just one thing, nor should it be.

Thank you, Cary, for creating this beautiful book that I can open, wherever I am, and be transported home. I'm very grateful.

QUESTION   **1.** As it relates to work, what are you grateful for?

I Love Change; I Hate Change

I love change. I especially love when something changes at work. I love new ideas and new ways of thinking about something. When someone suggests a new idea, I am the rabbit in *Alice in Wonderland* chasing the new idea down a hole. I become completely intrigued by the possibilities that the new idea conjures up. "What if we could …" is my favorite way to start a sentence.

This goes beyond a new idea about a work topic. If someone offers me a new job, or a new element to my current job, my first reaction is, "Why not?" This is who I am; I accept that I am too quick off the starting blocks, and if I were to spend a few minutes more thinking about what I was just asked, my reaction might be "why?" instead of "why not?" I once worked with someone at General Foods who told me, "My boss offered me the job as president of Maxwell House coffee. I was the head of marketing for Jell-O at the time. He told me I would move in three months. I went back into his office the next day and told him, 'You might as well move the rest of my body now, because my head left yesterday.'" This describes me, too. Once someone tells me I'm doing something else in the future, it's very hard for me to stay focused in the present.

I hate change. I hate change when it means I will no longer work with the people I work with every day. I get very attached to the people in my team. As I often say, work is hard. This creates a breeding ground for close relationships at work. As a team, you are battling the business dragons every day, and like modern-day knights of the round table, you form a fellowship that is extraordinary. This is one of the things that makes me exceptionally happy at work; without it, I'm miserable.

In the end, change is bittersweet. All the shiny new ideas in the world are no substitute for the joy I get from my relationships with my colleagues. However, life does not stand still. Each moment in time is just that, a moment. From this, I have learned two important things that help me with my love/hate relationship with change:

- Be present in this moment; it will not come again.

- Be happy now. No matter what the future brings, if I can be happy right now, it's enough.

1. How do you feel about change? Is your first thought positive or negative when faced with something changing?

2. Do you have a strategy for tackling change, whether it's good or bad?

Stop Judging

I attended Easter Mass, and one sentence from the priest's sermon struck home:

Stop judging.

It was like seeing an explosion of color before my eyes while I was watching a black-and-white movie.

What's your immediate reaction to the word "judge?" My instant reaction is negative: to me, judging implies criticism. It implies not measuring up to some criteria.

I considered *how* I judged something. To judge something meant I had to have an opinion about whatever it was. To have an opinion, I had to compare it to something else. And since I was judging something, it meant the comparison was usually unfavorable.

I took the priest's words at face value and added my own: stop judging, and it will eliminate a lot of negative energy. This can only be good.

A couple of days later I was sharing this thought with a person I had just met. She added, "Think of all of the times we judge ourselves, not someone else. Think about what we put ourselves through." I thought about what she said. How many times have I compared myself—unfavorably—to someone else? Did this make me happy or unhappy? It's not a trick question: it definitely made me unhappy.

Now take this thought and apply it to work. Are you ever happy at work when you judge yourself in comparison to others? Do these feelings foster a sense of collaboration or competition?

Stop judging. If I can live by these two simple words at home and at work, I know I will be happier and calmer. Where do I sign?

QUESTION   1. What connotation does the word "judge" have for you?

A Simple Exchange

The next time someone offers you advice, say "thank you" instead of "I know."

"I know" stops the conversation. It tells the person who offered to help, "You don't need to help me; I know this already." And I'm sure you didn't mean your response unkindly, and you weren't ungrateful for the proffered help. "I know" is a natural reaction—we've been saying it to our parents and teachers since we learned to talk! "Don't forget your coat; it's cold outside." "Yes, Mom, *I know.*"

"Thank you" gets me at least a smile and, often, another helpful comment. It also makes the other person feel appreciated instead of rebuffed. If you're looking for good ideas, saying "thank you" is nearly as powerful as asking good questions.

When I can remember to do it—and I don't every time; just this morning at work I responded, "I know" when I should have said, "Thank you"—I swap the two phrases.

QUESTIONS

1. Could you try swapping "I know" for "thank you"?

2. Are there other phrases you use that act as verbal stop signs?

We Are All CEOs of Our Families

I was talking to a dear friend recently, and we were discussing a variety of people-related topics: managing folks for performance, giving feedback, providing a support structure for people, and learning how to give encouragement at the appropriate moments.

All of these topics are very relevant if you're a manager at work—or the CEO of your family.

So many folks I know work so many hours. This blurs the boundaries between work time and family time, especially as our electronic gadgets turn into dog leashes tethering our work to us wherever we are.

It's natural that behaviors that are successful at work would also be helpful at home. One could argue that it's actually the reverse—behaviors learned at home are helpful at work. Maybe. I don't remember getting feedback as a kid, but I remember getting grounded!

I'm not kicking off a "chicken or egg" debate, but I will suggest that the skills from both worlds are transferrable. I like taking some of my management skills home, whether it's to effectively prioritize household tasks or to structure a decision we have to make. Equally, I like taking certain family skills to the office, and I think it makes the work environment richer. For example, I love celebrating an important milestone the same way you would at home—cake, balloons, and even better, as a surprise. It takes a little extra effort to organize this for someone at work, but the reward is a shared moment of happiness and celebration.

QUESTIONS
1. What's your favorite skill to transfer between work and home?

2. Which one do you find most surprising?

Like Your Boss

How do you choose your next career step? Are you clear about the criteria you apply when deciding about your next job?

I start with my boss.

Will I like her? Can I work with him? Can I develop a trusting relationship with her? Can I be loyal to him? Does she deserve my loyalty? Am I willing to *never* gossip about him? Do I respect her?

Don't get me wrong; no boss is perfect. Even the best boss will irritate or frustrate me at some point. But nine times out ten, will I be happy to see my boss's name on an email or incoming call? If I can't answer yes to this and all of the questions above, then I probably shouldn't take this job.

Sound extreme? Not for me. Work is hard. During my time in a job, especially a new one, I am going to make a lot of mistakes. I *never* want to call someone I don't like and tell them that I made a mistake. This is not to say it's easy to tell anyone that you made a mistake—it's not. But when you work for someone you respect and trust, it's easier to share a problem that you may have caused. Their first reaction will be to give you the benefit of the doubt—they know you did not intentionally make a mistake. All of my bosses have always jumped in and helped. No wonder I like them!

Now turn it around—are you a boss your employees like? Respect? Trust? Do you want your employees to come to you with problems? Do you bite their heads off if they do? I am sure you don't.

So maybe, "Will I like my new boss?" is not such an unusual criterion for choosing a new job after all.

QUESTION   1. Do you like your boss?

We're All Connected

I'm reading an interesting book: *Connected, The Surprising Power of Our Social Networks and How They Shape Our Lives* by Michael A. Christakis, MD, PhD, and James H. Fowler, PhD.

The authors looked at how our real-life social networks impact nearly every aspect of our lives, and they illustrate this phenomenon through startling facts. Did you know:

- "That your friend's friend's friend has more impact on your happiness than $5,000 in your pocket?"
- "That if your friend's friend's friend stops smoking, you will stop smoking?"
- "A person is about 15 percent more likely to be happy if a directly connected person (one degree of separation) is happy? The happiness effect for people at two degrees of separation (the friend of a friend) is 10 percent."

I am only halfway through the book, and the insights just keep on coming!

I think most of us intuitively knew some of this: it's easier to be happy when the folks around us are happy. However, I didn't know that someone out to three degrees of separation (the friend of a friend of a friend) could also make me happier. Gee, that takes some pressure off! Or does it?

I like to think it does. I like to think that if I'm happy at work, I can influence a wider circle (the friend of a friend of a friend) to also be happy at work, without even trying on my part. And better, having unhappy friends impacts you two percent less than having happy friends—the numbers will work in favor of being happy.

My "three degrees" and me are very happy.

QUESTION   1. How much influence does the mood of the people around you have on your own mood?

Goals Are Dreams with a Deadline

I don't go for a walk without having a destination in mind. I won't enjoy it. I don't like to walk just for the sake of taking a walk. I have never learned how to wander aimlessly. I can, however, walk for hours on end as long as I tie it to something I want, such as to get some exercise to burn off the cupcake I couldn't resist.

The same is true for my work. I need a destination—a goal—before I can put effort into something.

I set goals that I can accomplish within a certain period of time, and usually it's not too far in the future. I like milestones that are within reach. It makes me happy to complete a goal and move on to the next one; it's a great feeling of accomplishment, even if it might be something small.

My goals are part of a bigger picture—they are the stepping-stones to my dreams. Just like taking a walk to work off a cupcake is part of my overall program to stay healthy, the same is true for my work goals. (Maybe I should just stop eating cupcakes and save myself hours of exercise!)

QUESTIONS

1. Do you set goals at work that move you closer to your dreams?

2. Are they achievable within a reasonable time frame?

Sleep When You Can

I was talking to a colleague this week about sleeping. It's not such an unusual conversation to have at work when you have a global role for a big multi-national company. My "normal" is to travel two or three times a month between the U.S. and somewhere that is at least six time zones away from the east coast of the U.S., where I live. While I'm no George Clooney in the movie *Up in the Air* (the warrior traveler who prided himself on being the master of all things business travel), I do put my sleep cycle into a tailspin many times a month.

"Denice, how do you manage crossing the different time zones?" asked my colleague, who looked a little tired, having just arrived back in Munich from Boston.

"I don't really manage it well," I replied. "I've learned to sleep when I can. And I've stopped punishing myself for not being able to sleep when I think I should—if I can't sleep, then beating myself up for it doesn't make it better."

Sleeping well makes me happy. Just before I left my job in 2005, sleep was as elusive as the Loch Ness monster. I would wake up multiple times a night and struggle to get back to sleep each time. I would fall asleep exhausted at 9 PM, only to bolt awake at midnight, unable to get back to sleep.

In an odd way, learning to sleep—or not sleep—has been a good thing for me. Instead of fighting it and feeling frustrated by it, I've learned to accept that this is part of my work life and how my own body works. I have found strategies to make it better, such as:

- I never schedule any meetings when I first land in a new location. I block at least six hours between landing and my first event. If I had a sleepless night on the plane, I go to the hotel and sleep before I start my day.

- If I feel pretty good when I land, I stay awake. Normally, this is found time for me, and I am usually pretty efficient during these four or five hours when I expected to be sleeping at the hotel.

- When I get on the plane, if I feel sleepy, I go to sleep right away, even if it's 5 PM. I don't eat or have a drink, other than some water. Airplane food is *never* better than sleeping.

- I play Klondike on my BlackBerry. Go figure, but this makes me sleepy.

- And my number one strategy: I sleep when I can.

I'm pretty sure that many of my tips would not work for other people, but they work for me. And more importantly, they are indicative of my new attitude towards work: I've learned to accept this aspect of my work, rather than getting upset and frustrated by it.

QUESTION   **1.** Do you pay attention to your body rhythms and how they affect your work?

A Simple Act of Kindness

I flew recently on USAir from Orlando to Philadelphia. As often happens, I forgot my electronic book reader, a Kindle, in the seat pocket when I got off the plane. In the taxi on the way home, my cell phone rang.

"Is this Denice?" asked a man, whose voice I didn't recognize. "Did you just arrive in Philadelphia from Orlando?"

"Yes," I replied hesitantly, unsure of what this call could be about.

"I am holding a very nice Kindle that I believe belongs to you." (I had my business card with my cell phone number on it tucked into pocket on the cover.)

My first reaction was: Again? I did this *again*? Do you know how many times I've left (and lost) stuff on planes? Each time I do this, I swear I will never do it again and yet, for the umpteenth time, I've done it again. I must be the champion of losing stuff while I travel. I keep Apple in business on iPods alone.

The caller was a USAir captain, about to leave Philadelphia. He offered to send it to me, but I felt uncomfortable asking a complete stranger to do such a favor for me, so I suggested he give it to Lost & Found, and I would get it—all the time thinking, "What a hassle. This will probably take hours." He replied, "We can hold it at the gate for you." At first, I didn't understand. As I was already in a taxi, how would I get back to the gate? He explained that I could get a gate pass from a USAir check-in counter and come back to the gate.

I turned around and went straight back to the airport. When I got the call, I was in a taxi on the way home, so in order to do this, I had to leave my luggage in the taxi, with a driver I had just met twenty minutes before. I couldn't bring my luggage with me to run out to the gate, so I asked the taxi driver to wait, took his name and number, and hoped for the best.

I reached the gate, but no one from USAir was there, or in the waiting area. I then noticed a message on my cell phone. It must have rang while I was going through security.

"Denice, this is Penny," said the woman's voice. "The captain had to leave on his flight, but I have your Kindle. Give me a call and I can bring it out to you."

I called her, and as she walked toward me, I could see the errant Kindle in her hands.

"It's so kind of you and the captain to do this," I said. "I am about to travel a lot for the next several weeks, and it would have been a real hardship for me to not have this with me."

She shook off my thanks, saying that they were happy they could do this and that it all worked out. We walked out together, and I asked if there was a more tangible way I could say thanks. She said no.

Why I am telling you this story?

Their actions had an impact on me much more profound than the cost of replacing an electronic book reader. Both of these folks could have taken the path of least resistance and given my Kindle to USAir's Lost & Found—returning stuff left on airplanes to forgetful owners is not their problem. But they didn't. They took a couple of extra steps that, for me, meant a lot. It saved me hours of trying to remember where I lost it—at this point I had been on two planes, in two taxis and one hotel. I would have called each one of these places, and in the end, probably would not have gotten it back.

But much more than saving me time, this simple act reminded me that people want to help other people. We all get caught up in our day-to-day lives, which are hectic and busy, and no one ever has enough time. But when we make time for kindness—for a simple, kind act—the impact is astounding.

And here's another point: what do you think my impression of USAir is right now? We all are guilty of saying what's wrong with the airlines today—but here are two employees that prove what can also be extraordinary about airline travel. I bet, if I were to ask the captain and Penny, they would both say they are happy at work—you don't go the extra mile when you're unhappy.

QUESTIONS

1. When was the last time you experienced an unexpected act of kindness?

2. Or performed one?

New Job

Since June 2010, I have a new job: chief diversity officer for Siemens AG.

This is probably the first time in my working life where the *content* of the job is closest to the things I have passion for and love to do. For example:

- It's people-focused.

- It's about creating a new way of looking at things.

- It has a global scope.

- It's about building networks and communities.

- It brings people together who, in their normal workday, would not have any connection with each other.

Briefly, diversity is about inclusion in the workplace; it's about creating a work environment where anyone, regardless of background, gender, age, or sexual orientation, can contribute and excel.

But this isn't a lesson about diversity. It's about what it feels like to do a job that has, at its core, an element that is very different than a lot of corporate-type jobs. All of my prior jobs were jobs that most folks have had some understanding of. It was easy to explain what I actually did for work: chief financial officer, chief executive officer, programmer, consultant, and especially, my college jobs: short-order cook and janitor. It's much harder to explain what a chief diversity officer *does*.

After nearly thirty years of working, I am in a job that I can't easily explain. This feels a little weird. But while it feels weird, it also feels completely right.

I will try to explain what I mean by comparing my new job to volunteer work I did when I was fourteen.

When I was a teenager I would volunteer for a couple of weeks at a summer day camp for handicapped children. My sister, Missy, was profoundly retarded and had cerebral palsy. Missy went to a day camp near our home, and I helped out, together with my mother. I would play games or do small art projects with the kids. My training was having Missy as my sister, and I was under the close supervision of the camp leaders, who were special education teachers. Here's what I noticed: the special education teachers who worked with folks like Missy were extraordinary people. They were patient and kind; they were funny and dedicated. Special education teachers make very little money. Most of them work two jobs to make ends meet. I slowly began to understand that work could also mean doing something you had a passion for, something that you believed in and felt you had to do.

That's what my new job is for me. It's something I have a passion for, and while I may not be able to easily explain what I do, like I could when I was a janitor or a programmer, I am excited about this new challenge. Although I knew almost nothing about work when I was fourteen, I had already learned this very important lesson, and it's comforting to me that this lesson is part of the fabric of my new work more than thirty years later.

QUESTIONS

1. Are you passionate about your work, or at least some elements of it?

2. Think about the lessons you learned about work when you were first working. Are any of these true today?

Ask an Unexpected Question

I recently met ten colleagues I had not met before at Siemens Southern Africa. As I travel the world as the chief diversity officer for Siemens AG, I try to meet new colleagues that I would not normally come across in my day-to-day work.

Folks walk into these meetings a little apprehensive, because I do not specify an agenda or topics before our meeting. There's nothing for them to prepare. Here's why: we are all very task-oriented, and we rarely have thirty minutes during our day or even our week when we simply *talk* to someone. Every discussion, every meeting—well, at least the good ones—have objectives, goals, and expected outcomes.

I'm not suggesting we should depart from this behavior: they're important elements of working efficiently and effectively.

But I work better when I get to know the person sitting across from me. I ask, "What motivates you?" I leave it up to the person whether they want to focus on work or life topics. This doesn't mean that I need to know everyone's deep, dark secrets. I'm not a big fan of too much information. I *do* want to know what motivates someone, though. It's fascinating to me to learn why someone does what he or she does, especially at work.

Guess what? Most folks love to be asked this. This surprised me. I did not realize it was such a radical question until I observed the reaction it got when I asked it. People's faces light up, and they visibly relax. Sometimes I ask it another way: what makes you happy at work? I think the positive reaction is because they know they can answer this—they can get an *A*.

I encourage you to try it sometime. Ask an unexpected question; just be prepared to answer it yourself!

QUESTIONS

1. What was the most unusual question you were asked at work?

2. If asked, could you tell a complete stranger what makes you happy at work?

Add Light, Not Heat

When I was in South Africa, I had the pleasure to meet a woman who is a senior executive in a large German company.

We shared experiences, both professional and personal, and it was so much fun to make a connection with a new person. One topic led to another, and soon we were talking about how you get people to rally around a new idea.

"I always want light, not heat," she said as she described what a perfect discussion should look like. "So often, you are in meetings and the tone gets very heated. But does this move the topic forward?"

She continued, "I want to add light to the topic. Let's make whatever we're talking about clear to everyone, and then we're having the right discussion."

I thought about what she said and was struck by the truth of it.

"Heat" in a meeting usually means raised voices and people backing away, like you would from a hot stove. Add "light" and you have a completely different dynamic: everyone can see the topic more clearly and create a common understanding. *Everything* at work is easier when folks are starting from the same point.

I will apply this new insight to meetings I attend in the future. If the atmosphere starts to get tense, I will try to extinguish the heat, and add light—who knows, it might keep all of us from getting burned.

QUESTIONS
1. Think about discussions you have had that added heat, not light. Satisfying?
2. Will you do differently in the future?

A Simple Gesture

On December 15th, 2010, I hosted an all-day meeting in Munich, Germany, for 150 people at Siemens. None of the people attending report to me, they are all volunteers who have a passion and commitment for the topic we share. Each one of them has a very demanding day job, so attending this meeting required putting their own work aside for up to three days (because of travel) to participate.

The meeting had two objectives: to thank this group of people for work they have been doing for the company for a particular subject, and to inspire them to do more. To achieve these objectives, we brought in three outstanding outside speakers who are world authorities on their topics: Frans Johansson, Mahzarin Banaji, and Michael Gold.

Each of the speakers was spectacular; the first one raised the energy in the room beyond my expectations, and the following speakers added to it—all in all, a very successful day.

The attendees came from more than thirty-four countries, and my team took care of all of the logistics: arranging hotels, organizing transportation, and, frankly, any request that made the trip easier for our guests. This was no small effort, and we got many compliments on how well organized the meeting was. I work with a team of little rock stars!

In addition to the program, I wanted to do something that showed each of the attendees that I appreciated their contributions to the company, but I wasn't sure I would have time to speak to each one personally.

So I wrote each person a note by hand, thanking him or her for attending the meeting and saying that I was looking forward to spending the day with them. This took several days. Each card took a few minutes to write; multiply this by 150 and in total I spent about three days writing all of the cards. I looked at it this way: the trade-off of my time was small compared to the time each of them invests in our mutual topic.

Many people were astonished that I did this.

"Denice, I have to tell you—I looked at the note to see if it was printed on a computer to look like it was handwritten," said one colleague. I could only smile—imagining software that fakes authenticity.

"I promise you, if this was true, I would have picked software that improves my handwriting," I replied, laughing.

This simple gesture had an impact beyond my expectations.

Why am I sharing this with you? It's a reminder: something simple can have a big impact, especially if it says "thank you" and recognizes people as individuals. I knew folks would like the notes and be surprised by them, but I underestimated the impact they would have. I thought about it after the meeting and I realized that when you work for a very large company, it's easy to get a little lost. A simple but personalized gesture can help make even a very large company seem more like a family.

This makes me happy at work.

QUESTIONS
1. Is there a simple gesture you could make at work that would have a positive impact?
2. What stops you from doing it?

Setting My Own PACE

I often get asked how I transformed my addictive behaviors and negative beliefs about work, and even more importantly, how I sustain this transformation. Wouldn't it be easy to revert to old habits? Simple answer: yes, it would be really easy. (I still eat cupcakes!) I had to find an effective way to keep myself from sliding backwards toward being unhappy at work.

I learned to PACE myself.

P *is for Prepare.* I am prepared to face whatever might happen at work because I know what I want from work. I have come to understand what great work looks like in the context of a great *life*. I know where my work fits into my overall life picture. I was recently offered a new role in Siemens, and it was easy for me to accept it. Because I was prepared, I knew this role would be a great fit for me.

A *is for Ask.* I ask for what I want. I struggled to do this in the past. I would think: why should I get what *I* want? There must be someone else's needs ahead of mine; it can't possibly be my turn. On top of this, I assumed that everyone, including my boss and co-workers, should somehow magically *know* what I wanted without my having to ask. Of course, asking for what you want doesn't mean you'll get it 100 percent of the time—but I am 100 percent sure that if you don't ask, you will never get what you want.

C *is for Confidence (and Content).* I learned to stop doubting myself so much. I was often scared that if I didn't know something I should know, I would make a big mistake. Gee, do you think the world would end if I screwed up? Let's be realistic: very few corporate jobs entail life-and-death decisions. I knew the content of my job, and if for some reason I didn't know it, I could ask for help. In fact, I was an expert in the content of my job—so why *wasn't* I confident? This realization was liberating, and I quickly began to feel more confident. I stopped worrying so much, and in turn, I appeared surer of myself (because I felt more confident!). Now think about your own workplace—do you want to work with someone who worries all the time, or with someone who brings a certain amount of confidence to the task at hand?

E *is for Earn.* Earn your place at the table. Execute well, and your colleagues will seek you out for new opportunities. There is no better seat than the one you've earned. It gives you confidence, which in turn prompts you to ask for what you want, which you can do because you're prepared!

And best of all, your pace is up to you. Think of it as a long-distance race. Most of us can't run fast *and* far, but if we run slowly enough, we can run farther than we think we can. I learned this lesson nearly twenty-five years ago when a running coach from the New York Road Runners Club told me "slow down!" and in one night, I ran twice as far as I ever had before. Set your own pace, and I promise, you'll be amazed at the places you'll go and how much you will enjoy the journey.

QUESTIONS

1. Can you define what PACE means for you?

2. Of the four, which is the hardest for you?

Finding Happiness in Unexpected Places

I attended the Time CNN Fortune Global Forum conference in Cape Town, South Africa, at the end of June 2010. The focus of the conference was on the potential for economic growth in Africa.

It's the first time I have been in the same room with people who are important historical figures, such as Francois Pienaar, the captain of the 1995 South African rugby team, Mrs. Graça Machal, human rights activist, and President Clinton.

Each person was mesmerizing and captivating in his or her own way.

As I attended each presentation and met other attendees during the breaks, I found myself talking about all sorts of things *not* directly related to my work. I didn't realize how much I enjoyed this until I was telling my husband Michael about the conference.

"It was amazing and a little bit overwhelming," I said. "At one point, Mrs. Graça Machal came up to the group I was standing with and put her arm around my shoulder. I felt like I was getting a hug from history."

"And the women at this conference," I continued. "They were spectacular. The African women especially—each one is making a significant difference in her country by creating economic opportunities with a focus on social justice."

For the three days of the conference, I thought very little about my work. Yes, everyone I met asked me what I did. This was the only "work" activity I did for three days: I did not worry about catching up on emails or working on my open projects. I decided to just be in the moment, and this had a very unexpected outcome: I came back to work so motivated to do more.

Let me explain it this way: as I met people who were clearly impacting the world, not just their companies, I realized that the *impact* of my work was also important; that having an impact mattered to me. Will I impact the world the same way as Mrs. Graça Machal or President Clinton? No. To be honest, that's never been my aspiration. But doing something that matters is important for me to be happy at work and to be happy as a person.

This insight came from going outside of my day-to-day work. I can only encourage you to go outside of your own work to be happy at work.

1. Do you find time outside of work to look for things that will make you happy at work?

2. When was the last time you did this?

Remember the Moment

When you're happy at work, do you consciously remember the moment? Do you take stock of what's happening? Where you are? What you're doing? Who you're with? Do you put it in the happiness bank to use later?

I had to learn to do this. Until just a few years ago, I didn't really think about the happy moments when I was experiencing them. I took them for granted. Meanwhile, I held on to the unhappy moments. When I was unhappy, I would dwell on the source of my misery—going over it again and again—and frankly, making it worse.

I act very differently now. Not only do I take notice of the times when I am happy at work, I remark on it and bring it to everyone's attention. "Hey, how much fun is this? Isn't this a blast?" I always get rewarded with positive reactions from my colleagues, even if they're a bit surprised when I first make the comments. It is unusual, after all, to talk about fun moments at work.

Here's another point I've learned along the way: I never have fun at work by myself. I can only truly appreciate the happy moments when I have someone else to share them with. For me, this has been a very unexpected element of working with a great team—the fact that they amplify the happy moments at work. How cool is this?

QUESTIONS

1. Are you aware of the special moments in your workday when they happen?

2. What would happen if you expressed it out loud?

What Do You Do? Are You Really Your Job Title?

As a rule, we all know that Americans will ask "What do you do?" faster than nearly any other people on Earth. (Here's a test: the next time you meet someone new, *don't* ask them what they do for work. The conversation will go from zero to speechless in sixty seconds, I promise you.) Like it or not, very often what we do is perceived as who we are. We may even fall into that trap ourselves.

Is what you do the most interesting thing about you? Does your job title best describe who you are? Or are you like me, and you inwardly groan a little when the conversation kicks off this way? I'm not saying you shouldn't talk about your work—for many of us, this is a significant part of our lives—but the job title itself isn't why I work. My job description doesn't make me happy.

1. Think about when you first met the people closest to you, such as your partner or best friend. Did you spit out a job title and stop talking? I am certain you told your future partner a lot more about who you are, and what is important to you, than just your job title.

2. I would offer a different approach. Talk about what makes you happy at work instead of elaborating on your job title or a description of your company:
   - "I lead a team of talented, committed people, and we have fun working together, in spite of all of the challenges we face."
   - "Together with my team, we created a mission and vision for our department that anchors our goals to a common purpose."
   - "I solve complex problems as part of a leadership team."
   - "My work allows me to translate thoughts and concepts into beautiful visual representations of ideas that are important to people."
   - "I work for a company that can significantly improve the quality of human lives." (Having personally worked for tobacco and alcohol companies, it's nice to be on the supply side of the healthcare equation today.)
   - "I know how to expertly navigate the crazy cacophony of today's Internet. I help people get their messages out."
   - "I travel the world and work with people from many countries; I get restless when I'm not in an airport every two or three weeks."

3. I'm also sneaking in a related theme here: very few of us are individual contributors. I don't know anyone today who does not rely on other people to get their work done—we're all connected to someone else, even if we may not be the official leader of a team. Remember, you're the leader of Team You, and it has many members that contribute to its success.

4. Human beings are complex. There is no short answer for defining yourself. A job title, while descriptive, can be a crutch. Tell people about what makes you happy at work, and watch the conversation go to amazing places!

QUESTION　　1. Putting aside your job title, how would you describe yourself? Or your work?

Keeping Score:
The Metrics for Happiness at Work

Several years ago, I was the CEO of a company that provided administrative services such as payroll, accounting, and travel services for seventy thousand Siemens employees in the U.S. This is typically called "shared services," and many large companies structure their administrative services like this.

We measured if our customers were happy with our services by keeping score of our performance. We agreed with our key customers on a set of measures or metrics, assigned a value for each one, and tracked them monthly. We used little traffic lights on a single sheet of paper to provide a quick visual representation of how we were doing.

For example, if paychecks were paid on time 99.5 percent of the time, the metric would get a green. Less than 99.5 percent paid on time, and the metric would be yellow; and less than 97 percent paid on time would be red.

Every month we discussed the scorecard with our key customers, and as you can imagine, when every metric was green, it was usually a very quick meeting. Throw in a few yellows and reds, and the discussion took much longer.

But here's a funny thing that happened. We started to observe that even when all of our metrics were consistently green over time, our customers were not notably happier. In fact, the needle started to move: "Why is 99.5 percent good enough? Shouldn't it be 99.9 percent?" We talked about this phenomenon with colleagues from other administrative service companies outside of Siemens.

"I just don't get it. We do everything as we promised, and yet our customers are not happy," I remarked to Biswajit, who was my equivalent at a similar-sized shared services company.

Biswajit answered, "The same thing happened to us as we matured. In the early days, customers were a lot less demanding. Today, we operate at levels of quality, accuracy, and reliability I would have never imagined five years ago." And then he added, "We found a way around this—we tell our customers during our review meetings, 'If it's green, you must be happy.'"

Really? Is that the secret of happiness?

Now apply this to yourself. Can you use metrics to measure how happy you are at work? Probably not. I propose it's because we're not completely clear about what will make us happy at work on a day-to-day basis. We don't have our own traffic-light system. We're more likely to describe some future event that would make us happy at work:

- "I will be really happy as soon as my big promotion comes through."
- "When this big project is finished, I will be happy."
- "I know I will be happier when our office relocates closer to my home."

Here's the problem: we're waiting for a one-time event to happen. Does that mean you won't be happy at work until then? And sometimes, when the event comes, we are often not as happy as we thought. Maybe the big promotion came with a significantly increased workload.

My advice is this: be clear about what makes you happy at work *today*, and find a way to measure it. There's an old saying, "What gets measured, gets done." For example, I like working with my team, so every day I count the number of times I talk to my team members. Less than five times, I am having a red day. More than ten times, it's green.

Create your own traffic-light system. You will find that you will start focusing more on what makes you happy at work today. And remember, if it's green, you must be happy!

QUESTIONS

1. Can you measure what it is that makes you happy at work?

2. Can you define your own scorecard and traffic-light system?

Tips for Restoring Your Passion for Work

Work today demands a high level of energy and commitment. We're all working longer hours and, with the economy as it is, potentially feeling trapped. The boundary between our work and our lives blurs as we give more and more of ourselves to our jobs. Think about the requests you no longer feel you can say no to. Can you travel on a weekend for another critical meeting? Sure! No problem! Can you complete the hundred-page PowerPoint presentation by tomorrow at 8 AM? Sure! No problem! Singly, these requests are not the end of the world. It's their cumulative effect that makes us unhappy and frustrated. Because of today's uncertainty in the job market, we are reluctant to object or complain. We quietly soldier on and internalize our growing misery. When you add all of this up, we become less and less happy and passionate about our work.

Sound familiar? Are you so focused on holding onto your job you've forgotten what is important to you about your work? Here are some tips that can help remind you of what was important to you about work and maybe bring passion and a sense of optimism back into your work:

- Who we are is not what we do. What we do is an outcome of who we are.

- We are human beings, not human "doings." Although learning to stop is much harder than it is to keep marching, time off from work—even a little—can make life better.

- High-functioning people can tolerate a tremendous amount of stress and unhappiness for very long periods. If you recognize this, you can redirect this energy to the things you love.

- It's perfectly fine to "Find out what you don't do well and don't do it." (To quote Alf, the 1980s TV character.)

- Too often we feed the urgent while starving the important. Knowing the difference makes every crisis manageable and, often, no longer a crisis.

- No matter what is running in your head, you need to be present in the moment you are in, with the people in front of you. Too often our inner dialogues distract us, and we miss the important moment occurring right in front of us.

- Maintain your sense of humor; it will be much more important for your success than the cleverest financial analysis or marketing plan.

- Success is not always a result of careful, logical planning. Trust what your stomach tells you.

- Martin Luther King did not say, "I have a plan." Dream of a spectacular work life, and do everything in your power to make it come true.

Take the time to stop and think about these lessons—do they resonate with you? What are *your* key truths about what fuels your passion for work? You can use the list above, or create your own, and use them as talismans to ward off the discouraging and overwhelming negative moments at work.

QUESTIONS

1. Do any of the thoughts above resonate with you?

2. Can you create truths of your own?

Happy at Work

If there could only be one rule about how to stay happy at work, I would say it is: don't forget to *do* what makes you happy.

I know this sounds simple, but I find it isn't. All jobs have stuff that's urgent, and we often let this dictate our priorities. We keep pushing the things that are personally rewarding to the end of our to-do lists.

Our company holds management classes for people from all divisions, and recently I was invited to speak to a class that was focusing on leadership. It was after dinner on day two of the class. The setting was informal—thankfully, no PowerPoint charts were needed—and I opened with a few top-of-mind remarks about my view on leadership. Then we were off to the races! I spent the next two hours answering the participants' questions. They asked me lots of great questions, and it was just fun. For me, there are few things more fun at work than spending time with folks discussing a topic that I am very passionate about—leadership.

Why am I sharing this with you? It's hardly unusual that someone speaks to a management class within the company.

I was *exhausted* when I left my office to travel two hours to this event. I could have lain down on the floor of the conference center and gone to sleep. I had a million urgent things on my plate just then, and I could have easily used the six hours this was taking to tackle my never-ending to-do list; I had emails breeding like rabbits!

I knew this would be the situation when I committed to do this event. But I also know that this is one of the top three things that make me happy at work—I *love* the energy I get from being with the folks that attend these classes, because it takes me out of my day-to-day work. During the couple of hours that I am with them, I am present just in this moment. I have to be—they're all very smart, and I have to pay attention!

I *always* get more out of these sessions than I put into them, even when I have to juggle my own deadlines to fit them in. So, even though I knew it would be very hard to carve out the time to do this, I remembered what makes me happy at work, and I did it.

I drove home at 11 PM, and I was happy that I did this for myself; it reminded me that *I* have to keep *me* motivated and happy at work.

QUESTIONS

1. Do you know the things that make you happy at work?

2. Do you find time during your workday to do the things that make you happy at work?

About the Author

Denice Kronau is a twenty-nine-year veteran of the corporate world who takes you on a whirlwind tour of boardrooms, companies, countries, and cultures, sharing what she has learned about how to be happy at work.

Kronau began working full-time at sixteen. She has been a janitor, dental assistant, short-order cook, babysitter, auditor, computer programmer, audit director, chief financial officer, and chief executive officer. She sometimes regrets never having worked as a waitress—but she still has time!

Today, Kronau is chief diversity officer of Siemens AG. Her career has combined extensive shared services experience with senior leadership positions in finance, IT, and internal audit not only for Siemens, but also for multinational companies such as Diageo PLC, Kraft Foods International, and Altria—in both the United States and in Europe. She worked abroad for fifteen years, living in Munich, London, and Paris, and she still travels the globe regularly for her current job.

Kronau's passion is sharing with others her hard-won lessons about how to find happiness in the workplace. You can learn more about Denice and her insights at **www.DeniceKronau.com**.

Reading Group Guide

1. The topic of "learning lessons from unexpected sources" is a recurring theme throughout the book. Can you think of a lesson you learned from someone unexpected?

2. Denice shares many lessons that she learned when she was first working that stayed true for her throughout her work life. Is there a lesson that you learned early on that has helped you throughout your career?

3. Denice has held jobs ranging from being a janitor to being a CEO. She has learned lessons from each job. Can you think of an important lesson you learned from each of your jobs?

4. Having fun at work is another recurring theme in the book. Can you remember a recent event at work that was fun? What made it fun?

5. Imagine yourself at the end of your career. You are at your retirement dinner, and you are sharing some final thoughts with cherished colleagues, friends, and family. Finish this sentence: "Of all of the things that meant the most to me at work, I was happiest when …"

6. Knowing what you know now, if you could give career advice to your sixteen-year-old self, what would it be? How would it relate to being happy at work?

Turn the page to read an excerpt from Denice Kronau's next book:

From Boardroom to Beach Chair
How a Stressed-Out, Dog-Tired CEO Regained Her Passion for Work

Kronau tells the compelling personal story of her transformation from an exhausted, worn-out, and overworked CEO into a woman in love with work again. It is her story of discovery, or more accurately, rediscovery. She rediscovered all the things that she loved about work when she first started working, but somehow had lost sight of after twenty-three years. Her new book chronicles her journey from desperation to rejuvenation, finally realizing that work is like water: we need it to live, but if we allow it to overwhelm us, we will drown.

Coming in Spring 2012

Chapter One
Next Exit: Nantucket

The story I am about to share with you is a story about addiction, but not the usual ones—no illegal drugs, wild sex, or impulsive trips to Atlantic City. What I was addicted to were the behaviors that enabled me to climb up the corporate ladder—working endless hours, moving twelve times in twenty years for my job, putting myself about tenth on any priority list so I could attend the next "critically important" meeting, even if it meant traveling on yet another weekend. I was addicted to *doing* better at work, and when I did, I felt that the corresponding increase in responsibility meant I had to do *even* better, because more people now relied on me. And with each promotion, doing better took a lot more effort than it did before. I was sacrificing more and more. I worked even longer hours. Work took over my weekends; I stopped exercising—it took up too much time that I could spend on email and PowerPoint charts. I did it all in my quest to do my best.

I was a capable person, willing to work very hard, and my addiction delivered positive outcomes, so no one, including myself, knew I was slowly disintegrating. The only thing that kept me from completely falling apart was the relationship I had with my husband, Michael. It was the one area outside of work I was willing to invest in. Everything else—family and friends, my weight, and even my health—lined up third, fourth, and fifth behind Michael and work. And even my marriage involved a significant compromise: Michael and I lived in different cities because of our jobs, and we only spent time together on weekends.

No one can lead such a two-dimensional life and stay sane and happy. But, like all addicts, I had to hit rock bottom before I could change. While I was feeding my addiction, I lost sight of what I loved at work—which was working with people I valued and achieving significant milestones together. At the time I walked away from it all, work had become nothing but completing the next spreadsheet or PowerPoint presentation. Work had turned into an infinite series of tasks on my to-do list, and I could only see the lists growing longer and longer, with no end in sight. Quitting seemed like my only option if I was going to save myself.

The day came when I just couldn't do it anymore. The Energizer Bunny batteries had run out. The sixteen-hour workdays, the non-stop travel, and the constant blitz of urgent emails became all too much. Here's insanity: I would fly from New York to India—a fourteen-hour flight—for a four-hour meeting, then I would hop on the fourteen-hour return flight as soon as my meeting was over. Why didn't I just put the brakes on? Simply, I was too tired to think about how to fix me *and* deal with all the problems at work. Work won.

"I can't do this anymore," I said quietly to Michael, trying not to let the panic I felt in my stomach come through in my voice. He looked up from the sports section of the *New York Times* with a questioning expression. It was a Saturday morning in November, and we were standing outside a diner in suburban Chicago, waiting for a table for breakfast, part of our usual weekend routine.

"I have to talk to you about something important. I know we both like to read the paper in the morning, but I really need to talk to you *now*." I didn't think I could wait one minute longer to say out loud what I had to say.

Michael folded the paper and waited for me to continue, a little surprised at the interruption, since we both enjoy our weekend morning routine. He could see that I hadn't spontaneously burst into flames, so he was confused—how could it be urgent if I wasn't on fire or bleeding uncontrollably? I knew that he was secretly hoping that whatever it was would be quick, so I plowed right in.

"I can't keep working like this. I'm exhausted and I'm wearing out. I'm sad all of the time, and I no longer get the energy from work that I used to. I want to quit my job." There, the dead moose was on the ground right in front of us.

I could hardly look at him; I was shaking and in tears. "OK," Michael said, then pulled me toward him in a big hug. "If this is what you need, do it. We can afford it, and I don't want you to be this unhappy."

He made it sound so easy, and I realized it might be possible; instantly I felt months and months of worry fall away. I relaxed into Michael's arms and took a deep breath of cold, clean November air. I was calmer in that moment than I had been for the past three years. "I love you," I said.

Over breakfast, I tried to explain to Michael my overwhelming sense of despair, but I found that I just didn't have the words. I didn't know how to explain why it had taken me so long to decide to end a situation that was draining the life from me.

"Was there something that happened this week that you want to tell me about?" Michael looked at me expectantly.

"No, it wasn't any one thing. It's everything—everything makes me so tired." I had just ordered a Belgian waffle and was looking forward to the rush I get from carbohydrates and sugar. "To begin with, I'm sick of traveling. I'm sick of the pushing and shoving that comes with air travel. This week is typical—I will fly four times: tomorrow to Newark, Tuesday to Munich, Thursday back to Newark, and Friday, back to Chicago. Flying so much is making me crazy. I get really angry with the other travelers for being in my way, or hitting me with their suitcases, or bumping my arm during a flight. I know this is just a symptom of working long hours and not getting enough sleep, but it feels like this is all that my life is, and when I look ahead, I see endless flights with herds of jostling, traveling sheep, all bleating in my ear, and I just want it to stop." My eyes were welling up with tears again as misery flooded over me.

Michael reached out his hand to reassure me. "It's OK," he said. "You're quitting. So now it's up to you as to how you want to make this work. We'll talk about it when you're ready."

My brain and heart were racing, and I took a deep breath to keep from crying. Then suddenly a moment of pure calm descended. I knew what I needed to do—I needed to go home to Nantucket.

Have you ever been to Nantucket? If you have, you most likely understand why this would be the place to go when your life is falling down around you. If not, I will try to explain it to you. Nantucket is an island thirty miles off the coast of Massachusetts, an hour by fast ferry or just a quick hop by plane from the mainland. From our first visit in July 1995, I learned that you could travel to another world in just twelve minutes. You fly at fifteen hundred feet, and the island is in view from nearly the first minute after takeoff from Barnstable Airport on Cape Cod. On sunny days, the reflection of the sun on the ocean bathes the island in a golden haze, and Nantucket is a beautifully wrapped present waiting just for you.

The magic continues well after landing. For me, the best part is the air: as it fills my lungs, it somehow also quiets my mind—and this is tantalizing. Every time I'm on the island, I begin negotiating with myself as to when I can next come back and maybe stay longer. On our first visit, Michael and I explored the entire island, and discovering each new corner was like finding a favorite photo tucked away in the back of an old desk drawer. Nantucket is beautiful, but not spectacularly so. The natural vegetation is scruffy and very wild; it reminds me of my four-year-old niece's hair when she refuses to let her mother brush it for five days. The island has eighty-one miles of beaches, and while none of them are breathtaking or dramatic, they are each beautiful in a quiet, understated way. Let me describe Nantucket this way: when I first met Michael, I thought he was handsome—but as I fell in love with Michael, I realized that no face would ever be as handsome to me as his. Nantucket is like this. As I spent more time on the island over the years, its face became the one I wanted to see when I woke up every morning.

Nantucket's appeal sneaks up on you. After our first visit, Michael and I returned for vacations in 1996 and 1997 because we had both fallen in love with the place. The idea to buy a house there popped into my head one Saturday morning in January 1998 as we were reading the paper in bed. "At the rate we're going," I said to Michael, "we're never going to live anywhere. Our jobs keep moving us from place to place. We work in separate cities during the week, and we only meet up on weekends. But if we had a house on Nantucket, we'd have one place we could call home. Although we couldn't be there so often, when we were there, we'd love it." Ever practical, I added, "And we could rent it when we're not using it."

"Why not?" Michael said. "If this makes you happy, go ahead." The following Monday, I was on the phone to a Nantucket real estate agent, Marybeth, and within two hours she had faxed me nine listing sheets of houses on the market. Five months later, we owned a small house. At last we belonged somewhere; we had someplace to call home.

Seven years later, our house became my refuge when I took the option my stomach and brain craved—I quit my job and went home to Nantucket.

When I was younger, I never imagined that I would be president and CEO of a multimillion-dollar company. Before I joined Siemens in March 2002, I had worked for Kraft General Foods Europe and Diageo PLC in a variety of increasingly responsible roles, such as head of audit, financial controller, and director of IT strategy. But I had never served as chief executive officer, so the jump to CEO was exciting for me. Siemens is one of the largest multinationals in the world, and I ran its U.S. shared services company with fifteen hundred employees. On an annual basis, my company was responsible for issuing Siemens' seventy thousand U.S. employees their 1.9 million paychecks, managing almost $400 million in travel expenses, and handling many other back-office functions, including managing the ninth-largest commercial fleet in the United States.

Michael and I were living together in Germany when Siemens offered me the CEO position, which was based in northern New Jersey. I moved to Hoboken when I started the job; Michael stayed in Germany until four months later, when he moved to Chicago, where he was the president of a very large company. We had always had a long-distance relationship; even after over seven years of marriage, we had only briefly lived together in the same house. Both of us traveled so much for work that maintaining separate homes and commuting to see each other from where our jobs were based was normal for us.

And this was true until November 2004, when I realized my every waking hour was devoted to either work or traveling. On paper, my life sounded great, but the reality was very different. Sure, being a CEO was exciting—as I said, it was a huge promotion from everything I had done before, and when I accepted the job, I was eager for the challenge. Living apart from Michael was also OK; this was more of the same for us. But it had never occurred to me that the scope of this job would increase my travel to the point where I was often in an airplane four or five nights a week. My company's employees were in New Jersey, California, Florida, and India, and our customers were concentrated in more than ten states; this meant I was traveling at least twenty days out of thirty, and when I added the trips to see Michael, I felt like I lived at gate 103 in Newark Airport.

In truth, it wasn't just the travel that was getting to me. Let me give you a snapshot of one of my workdays at that time. It's 8 AM and I'm in my car, driving to my office in Iselin, New Jersey. I've been awake for only a little over an hour, and already I am so tired I could go back to sleep for the rest of the morning or even the rest of the day. The southbound lanes on the New Jersey Turnpike feel like a flattened hamster wheel—the faster I go, the more it seems like I am circling the same stretch of road—and driving eighty miles an hour only means that I am experiencing déjà vu faster and faster.

As I drive, I turn competing personalities on and off like a light switch. Philosophical Denice asks, "Why am I here?" Existing-in-the-moment Denice answers, "Well, I got on Route 1 and 9 going south, crossed the Pulaski Skyway, and entered the New Jersey Turnpike near Newark Airport." I keep up this internal dialog throughout the mind-numbing, forty-five-minute drive. I ask myself, "Why am I this tired?" Gee, could it be because I woke up four times last night and had trouble getting back to sleep each time? I forced myself to go for a walk in the morning (can I believe that I've gained forty pounds in the last year?), but the exercise feels like it's sucked the life out of me instead of providing the endorphin rush that fitness nuts rabbit on about.

I arrive at work, and I longingly look out of my window at a small strip of lawn surrounding the Siemens suburban office complex, wishing I could be outside. This is how I know I am seriously depressed—who longs to be outside in an office park in New Jersey?

My workday is one meeting after another, but I can hardly concentrate on any of them, since each meeting has that characteristic of the children's song "The Bear Went Over the Mountain": cresting one peak simply reveals the awful reality that there are endless mountains on the horizon. Because I run a service business, most of the things that cross my desk are problems for our customers, who are frustrated and angry. Good days are when I hear nothing, and as for praise, well, that is the holy grail of the service business and occurs with the same frequency as the seventeen-year cicadas.

This characteristic of our business was the same for all of my employees, not just for me, but as the leader, I felt a responsibility to make everything that had gone wrong better, and I put all of my evaporating energy into this. My employees, if I had asked them, did not expect me to fix *everything*. I expected this from me. This took a tremendous amount of energy, and although it was exhausting, it was part of my DNA—I didn't know how to work any other way.

Back to my typical workday: I leave the office about two hours later than I had planned, and it is already dark when I get back on the road to battle my way home. (And I ask you, is there any other way to describe driving on the New Jersey Turnpike? Forget *Survivor* on TV; I was voting all the other drivers off the turnpike on a daily basis!) I arrive home just in time to watch whatever stupid reality show is on TV at 10 PM and eat a pint of Ben & Jerry's Peanut Butter Cup ice cream for dinner. I am so tired that I could care less that eating ice cream undoes all the effort I put into walking sixteen hours earlier, and that the caffeine and sugar will keep me from easily falling asleep; yes, I am using the narcotic of ice cream to cheer me up—I am the poster child for comfort eating.

Finally, at midnight I drag myself to bed, and I check email on my BlackBerry just one more time before I turn out the light.

So if this was a typical day, why didn't I notice that my life was going off the rails? I did notice—I just thought that I could manage it, even if it was unmanageable. We all know the cowboys at work who thrive on the insane; I was as macho about working insanely as the toughest cowboy. I was also a perfectionist, which meant I was willing to work just a little longer at something in order to do my best. I hated deadlines, not because I couldn't live by them, but because it meant whatever I was delivering had a hard stop and I couldn't keep working on whatever it was. The time needed to work like this kept growing and growing, and somewhere along the line I stopped consciously choosing to put more time into work; I just did it. I traded time with friends, time for exercise, and time doing nothing to continue working on whatever project was at hand. The only time I protected was my weekends with Michael, and even that was impacted because of my crazy schedule, no matter how much I tried to limit my travel.

That was why my life as CEO became so untenable. I felt like I was not consciously making decisions or trade-offs: work always came first. Now, I understood that it was me who was allowing work to push to the front of the line, but it didn't feel like a conscious act back then. There is an urban legend about frogs that is used as an analogy for people's reaction to change. It goes like this: if you drop a frog in a pot of boiling water, it will jump out. But if you put a frog in a pot of cold water and very gradually bring it to a boil, the frog will stay in the pot and slowly cook. (Please, animal rights folks—I am not endorsing this experiment. It's an urban legend—just ask Google.) This anecdote illustrates how we can build up a tolerance to intolerable situations. As CEO, I was the frog in the pot being slowly brought to a boil, about to be stewed. While I was by no means suicidal, I had lost the ability to jump out of the pot. Yikes! How the heck did I get here?

When I decided to quit, I couldn't answer this question. And though I hated that I couldn't answer it, I took some comfort from the fact that I knew where I would go when I walked out on my job—I was going to Nantucket.

"Peter, it's Denice. I'm sorry to bother you at home on a Saturday, but I need to see you urgently. Can we meet on Monday?" Now that Michael and I had decided I would quit my job, I wanted it over with. So that very afternoon, after I recovered from my meltdown in the diner, I called my boss, Peter. My hand was sweating as I held the phone.

"Are you in New York?" Peter asked.

"Not until tomorrow afternoon," I said. "I'm in Chicago with Michael."

"Come see me at home after you land. By the way, what's this about?" Peter was a great boss but also a friend; he knew if I was calling him at home on Saturday that something was wrong.

"I have something important to talk to you about," I replied, not wanting to tell him I was resigning over the phone.

I could hear laughter in his voice as he said, "Well, I'm happy to talk to you on a weekend, as long as you aren't going to tell me that you're resigning."

It's true—silence *is* deafening.

Tears welled up in my eyes again, and for a moment I was speechless from shock. My emotions were pounding on my vocal chords like an arcade Whack-a-Mole.

"Actually," I croaked, "that is exactly what I am going to tell you."

I mumbled something about talking about it when I saw him tomorrow, hung up the phone, and looked at Michael. "I guess that didn't go according to plan," I blurted, still shaking.

"Think of it this way," Michael said. "Now you both have some time to absorb this. It will probably make it easier tomorrow."

While I wasn't convinced talking to Peter in person would be easier, I knew I had to find some way to explain this decision to him. Peter and his wife, Heidi, have been friends of Michael's since before I met Michael, and I knew them both socially for many years before I worked for Peter. Because he was a friend as well as my boss, I felt that I owed him a good explanation of why I was resigning, and definitely more than the standard two-week notice.

For the next twenty-four hours, I obsessed over what I would say to him. There was no middle ground—the question for me was simply whether or not to quit, never "How can I make my job better?" Still, although it came down to a black-or-white decision, I had to be able to explain to Peter, and everyone else, why I was taking such a dramatic step. Sure, the travel and long hours were stressful, but most people don't up and quit their jobs for these reasons. I had to give more than exhaustion as an explanation. The problem was, I had no energy to understand all of the root causes that were propelling me into the binary decision of "quit or stay"—and I didn't have any more answers to pull out of my survival kit.

New York was dreary and cold—not that matters could have gotten any worse at that point—when I reached Peter's apartment building late Sunday afternoon. I was very nervous about what I was going to say; the explanation playing in my head still rang hollow.

Even after thinking of nothing else for the last twenty-four hours, the only explanation I could come up with was: I am too exhausted to continue working. Was that it? That's the best I could do? I wished the elevator ride to Peter's floor would carry me to the future, when our meeting was already behind us and I had survived with some semblance of dignity. I was scared I was going to burst into tears and seem like an over-emotional, crazy person instead of one who had made a tough decision and was willing to follow through with it. I was afraid my words would not be sufficient when I met Peter face to face: I knew I was hanging on by an emotional thread when I started looking for insight from the Muzak version of "Send in the Clowns" playing in the elevator.

As I stepped out of the elevator, Peter was standing in the doorway to his apartment, waiting for me. Uh-oh. But he was holding a dishtowel in his hands, and from the kind expression on his face, I knew my friend was answering the door, not my boss.

We stepped inside his apartment. We sat in the living room, making small talk. For a few glorious minutes, it almost felt like a social call. I stopped gulping air and tried to slow my breathing to a normal rhythm.

Then Peter asked me, "Do you have to quit?"

"Well, I have to stop working, so quitting seems like the right answer," I said, a bit confused. How can you stop working if you don't quit your job? I continued, "I have been working full-time since I was sixteen. I'm forty-six. I am exhausted. I know this will sound illogical, but I am too tired to even know how tired I really am."

"Do you need to leave Siemens, or do you just need to stop working?" Peter persisted.

"I need to stop working, but no—this has nothing to do with Siemens."

"What about taking an unpaid six-month sabbatical?" Peter offered.

I was startled. This was very unexpected. The idea of taking a sabbatical had never even occurred to me. Everything up until this moment had been building up to a dramatic change—quitting my job—and I had already come to terms with my decision, and even felt a tiny bit proud for finally putting my own needs first. His suggestion of taking a compromise step felt almost like a letdown.

"I never thought about this. I've only been at Siemens for three years, so it never occurred to me that it would be an option." Suddenly, a small ray of sunlight broke through the cloudy gray sky outside of Peter's living room window, and my crushing sense of despair felt a little less overwhelming.

"Think about it," urged Peter. "We can make this work as long as you are sure you don't want to leave Siemens."

As Peter was making his offer—a way to solve my problem without taking an irreparable step—I realized this was another good example of how overwhelmed and exhausted I was feeling. Normally, I solve problems. Yet now I had a huge problem to solve, and my only solution was to quit, to walk away. It was hardly an excellent solution. At forty-six, I was too young to stop working—what would I do with myself for the rest of my life? And I couldn't afford to never work again, since I didn't have enough savings to cover forty years of living expenses. Peter offered me the lifeline that I could not figure out myself; instead of sailing into uncharted waters, I could change my life while holding onto the tie line of the big boat of Siemens. This made me feel immediately better.

I left Peter's house shortly after this, having agreed to take a six-month sabbatical and to give him enough time to find a successor for me. I hopped on the ferry from Manhattan to go home to my apartment in Hoboken, and although it was still cold and gray, I felt the opposite of the weather—it was sunny in my world for the first time in months.

Peter's search for my successor took several months. It was the end of May 2005 by the time my successor accepted the job, and I agreed to stay for one more month to hand over my responsibilities. While

I had hoped to leave earlier, knowing I was leaving gave me the strength to continue. But as my last day at work drew closer, I was getting very anxious. I was experiencing a constantly changing kaleidoscope of feelings, but only with dark colors. I felt guilty about leaving my team, but I also recognized that I did not have anything left to give them. Why not? Why didn't I have more? What was wrong with me? I also felt very sad—I was extremely close to the people I worked with in the three years I had been with Siemens, and soon our contact would be reduced—if we really made an effort—to the occasional email and sporadic phone calls. How could I leave them? What would my life be like if I was not with these people every day? And, to be honest, we really couldn't stay in touch; it wouldn't be fair to my successor.

Saying goodbye to my employees was extraordinarily difficult for me. I went to all of our U.S. offices in New York, New Jersey, and Florida, and at each one there were farewell parties and speeches and gifts. I knew I could not say goodbye without bursting into tears, so I let technology say it for me: I taped my farewell speech and played it during each of these events. As my goodbye video played, I looked into the audience, at all of the folks who had come to mean so much to me. At each goodbye party, I felt like I was attending my own funeral, and I left each tribute feeling loved, exhausted, and sad. Every final encounter with my employees was like the last hundred yards in a marathon; the goal was nearly in reach, and I prayed I'd get there before my heart exploded.

Let me give you one example. To this day, tears still fill my eyes when I remember a conversation I had with Suzie, one of the team who paid supplier invoices, during my last visit to the Orlando office, about two weeks before I stopped working.

"Hi, Suzie," I said as I walked past her cubicle. "How is baby Daisy?" Suzie had given birth a year before and had named her daughter after her closest friend at work. Coincidentally, I had been in Orlando on the day they held Suzie's baby shower, so I had attended.

"She's fine, Denice. Thanks for asking," Suzie replied. "And I want to tell you something," she continued. "Do you remember last year when you attended my baby shower?"

"Sure," I said. "It was a hoot, and I was happy to be included. Besides, I *never* turn down free cake."

Suzie smiled at my silly remark, but then she got more serious. "It's what kept me working at Siemens," she said. I must have looked puzzled, because she went on to explain, "I was very worried about my job because our division was not doing well. I had an offer from another company, and I was trying to decide if I should leave Siemens or if I should stay. I was getting more and more anxious, especially since I was about to go out on maternity leave. As I was trying to make a decision about all this, you attended my baby shower. I thought, if the CEO can take the time to attend a baby shower, then our business must be doing OK, even if it looks bad right now. At that moment, I knew that our business would succeed. I turned down the other offer, and I went on maternity leave much calmer and excited about coming back to work."

At that point, I couldn't see Suzie because of the tears in my eyes. The last three years had been very difficult—but the good things had been equally amazing, and I understood, in that moment, why I had been able to keep going well after my Energizer bunny batteries had run out.

Now multiply Suzie's story by a hundred, and you will understand what my last month was like. When my last day came, it was bittersweet and, honestly, just in time.

Ultimately, it took eight months to find my successor and for me to be able to finally leave my job, which I did in July 2005. When I finally left, the only nagging feeling I had was that I was walking away from something, not toward something. All my life I have been goal-driven; I don't even go for a walk without a specific destination or purpose. Yet now I was jumping off the roof of my life with no idea of whether I would hit concrete or the clear blue sea.

CPSIA information can be obtained at www.ICGtesting.com
Printed in the USA
BVOW040237020312

284270BV00003B/1/P